# Workplace Safety: Individual Differences in Behavior

*Workplace Safety: Individual Differences in Behavior* has been co-published simultaneously as *Journal of Prevention & Intervention in the Community*, Volume 22, Number 1 2001.

# The *Journal of Prevention & Intervention in the Community*™ Monographic "Separates" (formerly the *Prevention in Human Services* series)*

For information on previous issues of *Prevention in Human Services*, edited by Robert E. Hess, please contact: The Haworth Press, Inc., 10 Alice Street, Binghamton, NY 13904-1580 USA.

Below is a list of "separates," which in serials librarianship means a special issue simultaneously published as a special journal issue or double-issue *and* as a "separate" hardbound monograph. (This is a format which we also call a "DocuSerial.")

"Separates" are published because specialized libraries or professionals may wish to purchase a specific thematic issue by itself in a format which can be separately cataloged and shelved, as opposed to purchasing the journal on an on-going basis. Faculty members may also more easily consider a "separate" for classroom adoption.

"Separates" are carefully classified separately with the major book jobbers so that the journal tie-in can be noted on new book order slips to avoid duplicate purchasing.

You may wish to visit Haworth's website at . . .

## http://www.HaworthPress.com

. . . to search our online catalog for complete tables of contents of these separates and related publications.

You may also call 1-800-HAWORTH (outside US/Canada: 607-722-5857), or Fax 1-800-895-0582 (outside US/Canada: 607-771-0012), or e-mail at:

## getinfo@haworthpressinc.com

---

***Workplace Safety: Individual Differences in Behavior,*** edited by Alice F. Stuhlmacher, PhD, and Douglas F. Cellar, PhD (Vol. 22, No. 1, 2001). Workplace Safety: Individual Differences in Behavior *examines safety behavior and outlines practical interventions to help increase safety awareness. Individual differences are relevant to a variety of settings including the workplace, public spaces, and motor vehicles. This book takes a look at ways of defining and measuring safety as well as a variety of individual differences like gender, job knowledge, conscientiousness, self-efficacy, risk aviodance, and stress tolerance that are important in creating safety interventions and improving the selection and training of employees.* Workplace Safety *takes an incisive look at these issues with a unique focus on the way individual differences in people impact safety behavior in the real world.*

***People with Disabilities: Empowerment and Community Action,*** edited by Christopher B. Keys, PhD, and Peter W. Dowrick, PhD (Vol. 21, No. 2, 2001). *"Timely and useful . . . provides valuable lessons and guidance for everyone involved in the disability movement. This book is a must-read for researchers and practitioners interested in disability rights issues!" (Karen M. Ward, EdD, Director, Center for Human Development; Associate Professor, University of Alaska, Anchorage)*

***Family Systems/Family Therapy: Applications for Clinical Practice,*** edited by Joan D. Atwood, PhD (Vol. 21, No. 1, 2001).

***Diverse Families, Competent Families: Innovations in Research and Preventive Intervention Practice,*** edited by Janet F. Gillespie, PhD, and Judy Primavera, PhD (Vol. 20, No. 1/2, 2000). *Provides a portrait of the real lives and practical challenges of our nation's families as they face a new millenium. You will discover family adaptation and competetence in a variety of contexts and situations such as day-today issues of coping and survival, as well as major milestones such as sending children off to school, becoming a caregiver for a family member, and more.*

***Employment in Community Psychology: The Diversity of Opportunity,*** edited by Joseph R. Ferrari, PhD, and Clifford R. O'Donnel, PhD (Vol. 19, No. 2, 2000). *"Fascinating and instructive reading, indeed a must read for all community psychology faculty, students, and potential employers. Sixteen community psychologists offer compelling, diverse and unique perspectives on their employment journeys." (Keneth I. Maton, PhD, Professor of Psychology, University of Maryland)*

*HIV/AIDS Prevention: Current Issues in Community Practice,* edited by Doreen D. Salina, PhD (Vol. 19, No. 1, 2000). *Helps researchers and psychologists explore specific methods of improving HIV/AIDS prevention research.*

*Educating Students to Make-a-Difference: Community-Based Service Learning,* edited by Joseph R. Ferrari, PhD, and Judith G. Chapman, PhD (Vol. 18, No. 1/2, 1999). *"There is something here for everyone interested in the social psychology of service-learning." (Frank Bernt, PhD, Associate Professor, St. Joseph's University)*

*Program Implementation in Preventive Trials,* edited by Joseph A. Durlak and Joseph R. Ferrari, PhD (Vol. 17, No. 2, 1998). *"Fills an important gap in preventive research. . . . Highlights an array of important questions related to implementation and demonstrates just how good community-based intervention programs can be when issues related to implementation are taken seriously." (Judy Primavera, PhD, Associate Professor of Psychology, Fairfield University, Fairfield, Connecticut)*

*Preventing Drunk Driving,* edited by Elsie R. Shore, PhD, and Joseph R. Ferrari, PhD (Vol. 17, No. 1, 1998). *"A must read for anyone interested in reducing the needless injuries and death caused by the drunk driver." (Terrance D. Schiavone, President, National Commission Against Drunk Driving, Washington, DC)*

*Manhood Development in Urban African-American Communities,* edited by Roderick J. Watts, PhD, and Robert J. Jagers (Vol. 16, No. 1/2, 1998). *"Watts and Jagers provide the much-needed foundational and baseline information and research that begins to philosophically and empirically validate the importance of understanding culture, oppression, and gender when working with males in urban African-American communities." (Paul Hill, Jr., MSW, LISW, ACSW, East End Neighborhood House, Cleveland, Ohio)*

*Diversity Within the Homeless Population: Implications for Intervention,* edited by Elizabeth M. Smith, PhD, and Joseph R. Ferrari, PhD (Vol. 15, No. 2, 1997). *"Examines why homelessness is increasing, as well as treatment options, case management techniques, and community intervention programs that can be used to prevent homelessness." (American Public Welfare Association)*

*Education in Community Psychology: Models for Graduate and Undergraduate Programs,* edited by Clifford R. O'Donnell, PhD, and Joseph R. Ferrari, PhD (Vol. 15, No. 1, 1997). *"An invaluable resource for students seeking graduate training in community psychology . . . [and will] also serve faculty who want to improve undergraduate teaching and graduate programs." (Marybeth Shinn, PhD, Professor of Psychology and Coordinator, Community Doctoral Program, New York University, New York, New York)*

*Adolescent Health Care: Program Designs and Services,* edited by John S. Wodarski, PhD, Marvin D. Feit, PhD, and Joseph R. Ferrari, PhD (Vol. 14, No. 1/2, 1997). *Devoted to helping practitioners address the problems of our adolescents through the use of preventive interventions based on sound empirical data.*

*Preventing Illness Among People with Coronary Heart Disease,* edited by John D. Piette, PhD, Robert M. Kaplan, PhD, and Joseph R. Ferrari, PhD (Vol. 13, No. 1/2, 1996). *"A useful contribution to the interaction of physical health, mental health, and the behavioral interventions for patients with CHD." (Public Health: The Journal of the Society of Public Health)*

*Sexual Assault and Abuse: Sociocultural Context of Prevention,* edited by Carolyn F. Swift, PhD* (Vol. 12, No. 2, 1995). *"Delivers a cornucopia for all who are concerned with the primary prevention of these damaging and degrading acts." (George J. McCall, PhD, Professor of Sociology and Public Administration, University of Missouri)*

*International Approaches to Prevention in Mental Health and Human Services,* edited by Robert E. Hess, PhD, and Wolfgang Stark* (Vol. 12, No. 1, 1995). *Increases knowledge of prevention strategies from around the world.*

*Self-Help and Mutual Aid Groups: International and Multicultural Perspectives,* edited by Francine Lavoie, PhD, Thomasina Borkman, PhD, and Benjamin Gidron* (Vol. 11, No. 1/2, 1995). *"A helpful orientation and overview, as well as useful data and methodological suggestions." (International Journal of Group Psychotherapy)*

*Prevention and School Transitions,* edited by Leonard A. Jason, PhD, Karen E. Danner, and Karen S. Kurasaki, MA* (Vol. 10, No. 2, 1994). *"A collection of studies by leading ecological and systems-oriented theorists in the area of school transitions, describing the stressors, personal resources* *available, and coping strategies among different groups of children and adolescents undergoing school transitions." (Reference & Research Book News)*

**Religion and Prevention in Mental Health: Research, Vision, and Action,** edited by Kenneth I. Pargament, PhD, Kenneth I. Maton, PhD, and Robert E. Hess, PhD* (Vol. 9, No. 2 & Vol. 10, No. 1, 1992). *"The authors provide an admirable framework for considering the important, yet often overlooked, differences in theological perspectives." (Family Relations)*

**Families as Nurturing Systems: Support Across the Life Span,** edited by Donald G. Unger, PhD, and Douglas R. Powell, PhD* (Vol. 9, No. 1, 1991). *"A useful book for anyone thinking about alternative ways of delivering a mental health service." (British Journal of Psychiatry)*

**Ethical Implications of Primary Prevention,** edited by Gloria B. Levin, PhD, and Edison J. Trickett, PhD* (Vol. 8, No. 2, 1991). *"A thoughtful and thought-provoking summary of ethical issues related to intervention programs and community research." (Betty Tableman, MPA, Director, Division. of Prevention Services and Demonstration Projects, Michigan Department of Mental Health, Lansing)*

**Career Stress in Changing Times,** edited by James Campbell Quick, PhD, MBA, Robert E. Hess, PhD, Jared Hermalin, PhD, and Jonathan D. Quick, MD* (Vol. 8, No. 1, 1990). *"A well-organized book. . . . It deals with planning a career and career changes and the stresses involved. " (American Association of Psychiatric Administrators)*

**Prevention in Community Mental Health Centers,** edited by Robert E. Hess, PhD, and John Morgan, PhD* (Vol. 7, No. 2, 1990). *"A fascinating bird's-eye view of six significant programs of preventive care which have survived the rise and fall of preventive psychiatry in the U.S." (British Journal of Psychiatry)*

**Protecting the Children: Strategies for Optimizing Emotional and Behavioral Development,** edited by Raymond P. Lorion, PhD* (Vol. 7, No. 1, 1990). *"This is a masterfully conceptualized and edited volume presenting theory-driven, empirically based, developmentally oriented prevention. " (Michael C. Roberts, PhD, Professor of Psychology, The University of Alabama)*

**The National Mental Health Association: Eighty Years of Involvement in the Field of Prevention,** edited by Robert E. Hess, PhD, and Jean DeLeon, PhD* (Vol. 6, No. 2, 1989). *"As a family life educator interested in both the history of the field, current efforts, and especially the evaluation of programs, I find this book quite interesting. I enjoyed reviewing it and believe that I will return to it many times. It is also a book I will recommend to students." (Family Relations)*

**A Guide to Conducting Prevention Research in the Community: First Steps,** by James G. Kelly, PhD, Nancy Dassoff, PhD, Ira Levin, PhD, Janice Schreckengost, MA, AB, Stephen P. Stelzner, PhD, and B. Eileen Altman, PhD* (Vol. 6, No. 1, 1989). *"An invaluable compendium for the prevention practitioner, as well as the researcher, laying out the essentials for developing effective prevention programs in the community. . . . . This is a book which should be in the prevention practitioner's library, to read, re-read, and ponder." (The Community Psychologist)*

**Prevention: Toward a Multidisciplinary Approach,** edited by Leonard A. Jason, PhD, Robert D. Felner, PhD, John N. Moritsugu, PhD, and Robert E. Hess, PhD* (Vol. 5, No. 2, 1987). *"Will not only be of intellectual value to the professional but also to students in courses aimed at presenting a refreshingly comprehensive picture of the conceptual and practical relationships between community and prevention." (Seymour B. Sarason, Associate Professor of Psychology, Yale University)*

**Prevention and Health: Directions for Policy and Practice,** edited by Alfred H. Katz, PhD, Jared A. Hermalin, PhD, and Robert E. Hess, PhD* (Vol. 5, No. 1, 1987). *Read about the most current efforts being undertaken to promote better health.*

**The Ecology of Prevention: Illustrating Mental Health Consultation,** edited by James G. Kelly, PhD, and Robert E. Hess, PhD* (Vol. 4, No. 3/4, 1987). *"Will provide the consultant with a very useful framework and the student with an appreciation for the time and commitment necessary to bring about lasting changes of a preventive nature." (The Community Psychologist)*

**Beyond the Individual: Environmental Approaches and Prevention,** edited by Abraham Wandersman, PhD, and Robert E. Hess, PhD* (Vol. 4, No. 1/2, 1985). *"This excellent book has immediate appeal for those involved with environmental psychology . . . likely to be of great interest to those working in the areas of community psychology, planning, and design." (Australian Journal of Psychology)*

**Prevention: The Michigan Experience,** edited by Betty Tableman, MPA, and Robert E. Hess, PhD* (Vol. 3, No. 4, 1985). *An in-depth look at one state's outstanding prevention programs.*

***Studies in Empowerment: Steps Toward Understanding and Action,*** edited by Julian Rappaport, Carolyn Swift, and Robert E. Hess, PhD* (Vol. 3, No. 2/3, 1984). *"Provides diverse applications of the empowerment model to the promotion of mental health and the prevention of mental illness." (Prevention Forum Newsline)*

***Aging and Prevention: New Approaches for Preventing Health and Mental Health Problems in Older Adults,*** edited by Sharon P. Simson, Laura Wilson, Jared Hermalin, PhD, and Robert E. Hess, PhD* (Vol. 3, No. 1, 1983). *"Highly recommended for professionals and laymen interested in modern viewpoints and techniques for avoiding many physical and mental health problems of the elderly. Written by highly qualified contributors with extensive experience in their respective fields." (The Clinical Gerontologist)*

***Strategies for Needs Assessment in Prevention,*** edited by Alex Zautra, Kenneth Bachrach, and Robert E. Hess, PhD* (Vol. 2, No. 4, 1983). *"An excellent survey on applied techniques for doing needs assessments. . . It should be on the shelf of anyone involved in prevention." (Journal of Pediatric Psychology)*

***Innovations in Prevention,*** edited by Robert E. Hess, PhD, and Jared Hermalin, PhD* (Vol. 2, No. 3, 1983). *An exciting book that provides invaluable insights on effective prevention programs.*

***Rx Television: Enhancing the Preventive Impact of TV,*** edited by Joyce Sprafkin, Carolyn Swift, PhD, and Robert E. Hess, PhD* (Vol. 2, No. 1/2, 1983). *"The successful interventions reported in this volume make interesting reading on two grounds. First, they show quite clearly how powerful television can be in molding children. Second, they illustrate how this power can be used for good ends." (Contemporary Psychology)*

***Early Intervention Programs for Infants,*** edited by Howard A. Moss, MD, Robert E. Hess, PhD, and Carolyn Swift, PhD* (Vol. 1, No. 4, 1982). *"A useful resource book for those child psychiatrists, paediatricians, and psychologists interested in early intervention and prevention." (The Royal College of Psychiatrists)*

***Helping People to Help Themselves: Self-Help and Prevention,*** edited by Leonard D. Borman, PhD, Leslie E. Borck, PhD, Robert E. Hess, PhD, and Frank L. Pasquale* (Vol. 1, No. 3, 1982). *"A timely volume . . . a mine of information for interested clinicians, and should stimulate those wishing to do systematic research in the self-help area." (The Journal of Nervous and Mental Disease)*

***Evaluation and Prevention in Human Services,*** edited by Jared Hermalin, PhD, and Jonathan A. Morell, PhD* (Vol. 1, No. 1/2, 1982). *Features methods and problems related to the evaluation of prevention programs.*

# Workplace Safety: Individual Differences in Behavior

Alice F. Stuhlmacher
Douglas F. Cellar

Editors

*Workplace Safety: Individual Differences in Behavior* has been co-published simultaneously as *Journal of Prevention & Intervention in the Community*, Volume 22, Number 1 2001.

The Haworth Press, Inc.
New York • London • Oxford

*Workplace Safety: Individual Differences in Behavior* has been co-published simultaneously as *Journal of Prevention & Intervention in the Community*™, Volume 22, Number 1 2001.

The development, preparation, and publication of this work has been undertaken with great care. However, the publisher, employees, editors, and agents of The Haworth Press and all imprints of The Haworth Press, Inc., including The Haworth Medical Press® and Pharmaceutical Products Press®, are not responsible for any errors contained herein or for consequences that may ensue from use of materials or information contained in this work. Opinions expressed by the author(s) are not necessarily those of The Haworth Press, Inc.

The Haworth Press, Inc., 10 Alice Street, Binghamton, NY 13904-1580 USA

Cover design by Thomas J. Mayshock Jr.

**Library of Congress Cataloging-in-Publication Data**

Workplace Safety / Alice F. Stuhlmacher, Douglas F. Cellar, editors.
     p. cm.
    Includes bibliographical references and index.
    ISBN 0-7890-1355-X (alk. paper)–ISBN 0-7890-1356-8 (alk. paper)
    1. Industrial safety. 2. Industrial safety –Psychological aspects. 3. Industrial hygiene. I. Stuhlmacher, Alice F. II. Cellar, Douglas F. III. Journal of prevention & intervention in the community.

T55.W668 2001
363.1–dc21
                                            2001039149

# Indexing, Abstracting & Website/Internet Coverage

This section provides you with a list of major indexing & abstracting services. That is to say, each service began covering this periodical during the year noted in the right column. Most Websites which are listed below have indicated that they will either post, disseminate, compile, archive, cite or alert their own Website users with research-based content from this work. (This list is as current as the copyright date of this publication.)

Abstracting, Website/Indexing Coverage ........ Year When Coverage Began

- *Behavioral Medicine Abstracts* ........................ 1996

- *BUBL Information Service, an Internet-based Information Service for the UK higher education community <URL:http://bubl.ac.uk/>* ........................ 1996

- *CNPIEC Reference Guide: Chinese National Directory of Foreign Periodicals* ........................ 1996

- *EMBASE/Excerpta Medica Secondary Publishing Division <URL: http://www.elsevier.nl>* ........................ 1999

- *e-psyche, LLC <www.e-psyche.net>* ........................ 2001

- *Family Studies Database (online and CD/ROM) <www.nisc.com>* ........................ 1996

- *FINDEX <www.publist.com>* ........................ 1999

- *Gay & Lesbian Abstracts <www.nisc.com>* ........................ 2000

(continued)

(continued)

*Special Bibliographic Notes related to special journal issues (separates) and indexing/abstracting:*

- indexing/abstracting services in this list will also cover material in any "separate" that is co-published simultaneously with Haworth's special thematic journal issue or DocuSerial. Indexing/abstracting usually covers material at the article/chapter level.
- monographic co-editions are intended for either non-subscribers or libraries which intend to purchase a second copy for their circulating collections.
- monographic co-editions are reported to all jobbers/wholesalers/approval plans. The source journal is listed as the "series" to assist the prevention of duplicate purchasing in the same manner utilized for books-in-series.
- to facilitate user/access services all indexing/abstracting services are encouraged to utilize the co-indexing entry note indicated at the bottom of the first page of each article/chapter/contribution.
- this is intended to assist a library user of any reference tool (whether print, electronic, online, or CD-ROM) to locate the monographic version if the library has purchased this version but not a subscription to the source journal.
- individual articles/chapters in any Haworth publication are also available through the Haworth Document Delivery Service (HDDS).

## ABOUT THE EDITORS

**Alice F. Stuhlmacher, PhD,** received her doctorate from Purdue University in Industrial/Organizational Psychology. She currently serves as Associate Professor at DePaul University in Chicago. In addition to safety, her research includes work on gender issues, unions, negotiation and decision-making in the workplace.

**Douglas F. Cellar, PhD,** received his doctorate from the University of Akron in Industrial/Organizational Psychology and currently serves as Associate Professor at DePaul University in Chicago. In addition to safety, his research interests include work motivation, organizational training, and assessment.

# Workplace Safety:
# Individual Differences in Behavior

## CONTENTS

# The Role of Individual Differences in Understanding and Predicting Workplace Safety

Alice F. Stuhlmacher
Douglas F. Cellar

DePaul University

Workplace safety is a critical topic for study. An alarming number of workplace safety accidents and incidents occur daily. For example, Loughlin, Hepburn, and Barling (1995) estimated that in the United States *each year*, there are 100,000 work-related accident or disease fatalities, 400,000 workers that become disabled, and 6 million employees suffering workplace injuries. Few areas in psychology have such pressing societal needs and organizational costs to be addressed.

It is clear that in order to increase and promote safe behavior, researchers need to understand the predictors and correlates of safe and unsafe behavior. Understanding and predicting safe and unsafe behavior is not a new idea in psychology. Community psychologists have studied safe and unsafe behaviors relating to both physical health (e.g., smoking, safe sex), and mental health (e.g., stress). Similarly, Industrial/Organizational psychologists have studied safety issues,

Address correspondence to: Alice F. Stuhlmacher, DePaul University, Department of Psychology, 2219 N. Kenmore Avenue, Chicago, IL 60614 (E-mail: *astuhlma@wppost.depaul.edu*).

[Haworth co-indexing entry note]: "The Role of Individual Differences in Understanding and Predicting Workplace Safety." Stuhlmacher, Alice F., and Douglas F. Cellar. Co-published simultaneously in *Journal of Prevention & Intervention in the Community* (The Haworth Press, Inc.) Vol. 22, No. 1, 2001, pp. 1-3; and: *Workplace Safety: Individual Differences in Behavior* (ed: Alice F. Stuhlmacher, and Douglas F. Cellar) The Haworth Press, Inc., 2001, pp. 1-3. Single or multiple copies of this article are available for a fee from The Haworth Document Delivery Service [1-800-342-9678, 9:00 a.m. - 5:00 p.m. (EST). E-mail address: getinfo@haworthpressinc.com].

*1*

often as ergonomic or physiological problems (e.g., McCormick & Sanders, 1982) or as behavioral-motivational problems (e.g., Fox, Hopkins, & Anger, 1987; Komaki, Barwick, & Scott, 1978; Ludwig & Geller, 1997). The work compiled in this collection presents a new perspective on safety behaviors–that of understanding individual differences in the workplace.

This volume addresses the topic theoretically as well as with empirical research in the laboratory and the field. Our authors offer perspectives in two key areas. The first is in how safety is defined and measured. This measurement and definition is critical in understanding the tasks, incidents, worker activities, and abilities related to safety. Second, the authors consider a variety of individual differences (e.g., gender, job knowledge, conscientiousness, self-efficacy, risk avoidance, stress tolerance, locus of control) that may be important in creating safety interventions and improving the selection and training of employees.

In the first paper, Carlla Smith and colleagues consider the importance of measurement in understanding worker abilities and defining safety behaviors. Empirical data from two organizations are presented indicating that important relationships may be missed if only recorded accidents are used as an index of an individual's safety behavior. The second paper, by Doverspike and Blumental, considers the neglected issue of gender differences in safety definitions and research. They present arguments for considering not only physical safety but broadening the definition of safety to include responsibility for the safety of others and psychological safety. The third paper by Arthur and Doverspike discusses an empirical study on the relationship between personality variables, job knowledge, and accident involvement. Their research suggests that driver knowledge is less influential in predicting crashes than personality, and in particular, conscientiousness. Following this, Cellar, Nelson, Yorke and Bauer present a related study examining the five-factor personality model in predicting safety behavior. They suggest that prevention efforts may want to target behaviors related to conscientiousness. The fifth paper (Forcier, Walters, Brasher, & Jones) presents a model of safety consciousness and a review of research regarding an inventory to measure the three dimensions related to the construct of safety consciousness. In the sixth paper, Hantula and colleagues examine the types of safety hazards and monetary costs of accidents in the public spaces of stores and malls with an interest in possible interventions to reduce the number of accidents. This volume concludes with a practitioner's perspective on individual differences in safety behavior.

Safety is a real world problem. The research presented in this collection addresses this problem and demonstrates the strengths of scientist-practitioner inquiry. Thus, readers will find these papers a meaningful foundation for both explaining safety behavior and implementing practical interventions.

## REFERENCES

Fox, M. L., Hopkins, B. L., & Anger, W. K. (1987). The long term effects of a token economy on safety performance in open-pit mining. *Journal of Applied Behavior Analysis*, *20*, 215-224.

Komaki, J. L., Barwick, K. D., & Scott, L. R. (1978). A behavioral approach to occupational safety: Pinpointing and reinforcing safe performance in a food manufacturing plant. *Journal of Applied Psychology*, *63*, 434-445.

Loughlin, C. A., Hepburn, C. G., & Barling, J. (1995). Changing future managers' attitudes toward occupational health and safety. In L. E. Tetrick & J. Barling, (eds.) *Changing employment relations* (pp. 145-514). Washington, DC: American Psychological Association.

Ludwig, T. T., & Geller, E. E. (1997). Assigned versus participative goals setting and response generalization: Managing injury control among professional pizza deliverers. *Journal of Applied Psychology*, 82, 253-261.

McCormick, E. J., & Sanders, M. S. (1982). *Human factors in engineering and design*. New York: McGraw-Hill.

# A Comprehensive Method
# for the Assessment of Industrial
# Injury Events

Carlla S. Smith
Gary S. Silverman
T. M. Heckert
M. H. Brodke
B. E. Hayes
M. K. Silverman
L. K. Mattimore

Bowling Green University

**SUMMARY.** Because work-related injuries are infrequent and often poorly documented, injury event operationalizations beyond recorded rates would be beneficial. This study describes a method that uses self-reported and recorded events.

Researchers interviewed workers and obtained recorded events from personnel files to develop the near miss and unreported injury events measures. The self-reported event measures, with other safety variables and demographics, were then administered to two groups of plant

Carlla S. Smith, PhD, Gary S. Silverman, DEnv, T. M. Heckert, PhD, M. H. Brodke, PhD, B. E. Hayes, PhD, M. K. Silverman, PhD, and L. K. Mattimore, PhD, are all affiliated with Bowling Green State University.

Address correspondence to: Carlla S. Smith, Department of Psychology, Bowling Green State University, Bowling Green, OH 43403.

This study was supported by a Faculty Research Major Grant Award (#128-8533) from Bowling Green State University.

[Haworth co-indexing entry note]: "A Comprehensive Method for the Assessment of Industrial Injury Events." Smith et al. Co-published simultaneously in *Journal of Prevention & Intervention in the Community* (The Haworth Press, Inc.) Vol. 22, No. 1, 2001, pp. 5-20; and: *Workplace Safety: Individual Differences in Behavior* (ed: Alice F. Stuhlmacher, and Douglas F. Cellar) The Haworth Press, Inc., 2001, pp. 5-20. Single or multiple copies of this article are available for a fee from The Haworth Document Delivery Service [1-800-342-9678, 9:00 a.m. - 5:00 p.m. (EST). E-mail address: getinfo@haworthpressinc.com].

5

workers (N = 115 and N = 120). Results indicated that self-reported events differed from recorded events and are related to other work injury variables (e.g., work hazards, overtime). An expanded safety protocol such as this one may provide additional tools to investigate the injury event process. *[Article copies available for a fee from The Haworth Document Delivery Service: 1-800-342-9678. E-mail address: <getinfo@haworth pressinc.com> Website: <http://www.HaworthPress.com> © 2001 by The Haworth Press, Inc. All rights reserved.]*

**KEYWORDS.** Injury events, recorded injury events, safety methods, self-reported injury events, work safety

Because industrial mishaps involving equipment damage and/or personal injury are relatively rare events (Chapanis, 1959), researchers are typically faced with methodological and statistical problems in collecting, analyzing, and interpreting these types of data. For example, the low base rate of industrial injuries per worker often necessitates collecting injury event data over long time periods to increase statistical power and using non-parametric statistical tests to compensate for the highly skewed data. Although statistical options such as non-parametric analyses and normalization formulae exist, these tests often lack sufficient statistical power to find significant effects (especially with small samples sizes) and/or transform the data into a form very different from the original data.

Beyond the straightforward statistical/methodological problems associated with collecting injury events and associated injuries, other, less apparent issues probably have an even greater impact on the accuracy of injury-related data. Under-reporting work conditions related to injuries is quite common. Researchers who studied Occupational Safety and Health Administration (OSHA) logs have found that work-related injuries and illnesses and lost work days are frequently not recorded (Oleinick et al., 1993), and only 75% of those organizations required to keep an OSHA log comply (Seligman, Sieber, Pederson, Sundin, & Frazier, 1988). In some situations, workers may not have reported work injuries to the worker compensation system because they received treatment from company-based or external insurance and disability programs (Fingar, Hopkins, & Nelson, 1992; Murphy, Sorock, Courtney, Webster, & Leamon, 1996).

Several studies have directly demonstrated the failure of OSHA and/or company-based reporting systems. For example, Weddle's

(1996) investigation of hospital environmental service workers (N = 372) showed that, of the workers who experienced injuries in the previous year (n = 108), 38.9% did not report their injuries. Weddle found that older and longer tenured workers were more likely to have not reported their injuries. The most commonly cited reason for not reporting was that the injury was minor; however, many of these injuries needed medical care (64.4%) or required lost work time (44.1%).

Pransky, Snyder, Dembe, and Himmelstein (1999) used a case study approach in multiple industries to examine the extent of under-reporting work-related injuries and the reasons behind them. Questionnaires and interviews were administered to 110 workers in similar jobs and their management at three industrial facilities. Less than 5% of the workers reported a work-related injury or illness within the previous years, although 50% or more experienced work-related symptoms or persistent problems, and 30% reported lost time or work restrictions because of a work-related injury or illness. Some of the reasons for which workers reported these discrepancies included fear of (management) reprisal, and lack of management responsiveness. Managers reported administrative barriers to accurate reporting, mostly to achieve pre-set safety goals. For these reasons, Pransky et al. (1999) recommended that, because of the widespread inaccuracy of recorded injury data, worker surveys and symptoms reports be used to provide more accurate and timely accounts.

The previous discussion has aptly demonstrated that many organizational reporting systems are replete with omissions and spurious information. This situation is of even greater concern because many safety training programs are based on data obtained from company records. For these reasons, operationalizations of industrial injury events beyond event rates from personnel records (recorded events) would be beneficial to safety researchers and practitioners. The present study presents the development and assessment (validity) of an industrial injury research method for the manufacturing industry that uses near (or near-miss) injury events and unreported injury events in addition to recorded injury events.

This research consisted of two phases. In the first phase, a small group of workers was interviewed with structured interviews to obtain near miss events. These data were used to construct a near-injury events self-report measure. Data on recorded events and resulting injuries were also collected from personnel records and interviews. This information was used to construct an unreported events and injuries self-report measure. In the second phase, the near events and unreported events measures, along with relevant demographic and validity (e.g., job safety and hazards) measures, were administered to two samples of industrial workers. Both the self-report measures and the recorded events data were used to obtain a more realistic and comprehensive picture of the injury event process in the two plants.

## METHOD

### Participants

Sample 1 (Plastics Plant): The final sample consisted of 115 shift-workers (48% of the total production workforce) across three permanent (fixed) shifts in a non-unionized plant that manufactures small plastic parts. Company tenure averaged seven years, nine months, and the average age of the workers was 37 years. Shiftworkers reported that they worked an average of 6.7 hours of overtime per week.

Sample 2 (Glass Plant): The final sample consisted of 120 shift-workers (25% of the total production workforce) on a weekly rotating shift cycle in a unionized glass manufacturing plant. Due to personnel cutbacks according to seniority, the production workforce was older, ranging from 43-62 years, with more than half being over 50. Tenure with the company ranged from eight to over 42 years, with 93% of the shiftworkers having over 24 years of tenure.

Multiple factors affected the response rate in the plants. Both plants suffered from poor labor-management relationships. However, the union-management relationship in the glass plant was particularly adversarial, reflecting the lower participation rate. Other factors, however, had an impact, such as scheduling difficulties, lack of communication between management and floor supervisors, and inadequate plant facilities for survey administration.

### Phase 1: Injury Event Measures Development

Please note the term "injury event" is used here instead of the common term "accident" because "accident" connotes some level of personal blame, whereas "injury event" is a more generic term. Also, the focus of the present study is on these injury events, not the related injuries or shift differences in either. The injuries themselves (including shift differences in injuries) are the central topic in a related article by Smith et al. (1997).

*Near-injury events.* Near events are defined here as "a situation which could potentially result in injury or damage" (Chapanis, 1959). Approximately 25 dimensions that assess unsafe behaviors were used as core dimensions in the present study (see Tarrants, 1980). In addition to the core dimensions, near events data were gathered through the use of the critical incident technique (Flanagan, 1954). Using the critical incident technique, an interviewer asked a stratified sample of participant observers (workers) to recall and describe unsafe behaviors they had made or had observed in their work environment. A structured interview similar to the one proposed by Tarrants (1980) was used to gather these data.

The data reported in the critical incidents interviews were used to develop the near events measure for the next phase. Respondents were asked to indicate the number of different types of near events they had experienced during the past year, the shift they were on when each event occurred, and their best estimate of the likelihood that future injury might result from the near event. The one-year time span was adopted to minimize distortion of these subjective estimates from historical events. Open-ended questions about near events not covered in the questionnaire were also included. An example of selected items from the near events measure from one organization is provided in Table 1.

*Recorded injury events.* The incidence rate of recorded injury events was assessed. Our definition of injury events covered the spectrum from major events with serious personal injury (and/or extensive equipment/facility damage) to minor events with slight or no personal injury (and/or slight or no equipment/facility damage). Historical data were obtained from personnel records for the previous five years; this degree of aggregation is consistent with prior injury research (e.g., Levin, Oler, & Whiteside, 1985; Wojtczak-Jaroszowa, & Jarosz, 1987). The number of recorded injury events (total and by year) was calculated for each worker who participated in the study. Injury event rate was calculated by assessing the number of events within a given time period and by shift. The BLS statistics were not used here because

## TABLE 1. Selected Items from Near Injury Events Questionnaire

Below is a list of almost or near accidents that have been reported by workers at plants like____. A near accident is something that <u>could have caused an injury but did not.</u> Describe any near accidents that have happened to you. For each near accident, please tell us <u>your best estimate</u> of how often this near accident has happened to you in the <u>past 12 months</u> on each shift (1 = day, 2 = afternoon, and 3 = midnight shifts). Also, tell us how likely it would be that an injury could result from this near accident (using the list of letters below).

INJURY LIKELIHOOD
A = no chance of injury
B = little chance of injury
C = fair chance of injury
D = great chance of injury

<u>NEAR ACCIDENT</u>

**I almost had an accident when I adjusted
a machine while its parts were still moving.**
    number of times on shift 1_____
    number of times on shift 2_____         Injury likelihood._____
    number of times on shift 3_____         (use letters above)

**I almost had an accident when I operated
a machine without a safety guard.**
    number of times on shift 1_____
    number of times on shift 2_____         Injury likelihood._____
    number of times on shift 3_____         (use letters above)

**I almost had an accident when I slipped
on something on the floor.**
    number of times on shift 1_____
    number of times on shift 2_____         Injury likelihood._____
    number of times on shift 3_____         (use letters above)

**I almost had an accident when I
participated in horseplay in the plant.**
    number of times on shift 1_____
    number of times on shift 2_____         Injury likelihood._____
    number of times on shift 3_____         (use letters above)

**I almost had an accident when I lost control
of the tool or equipment that I was using.**
    number of times on shift 1_____
    number of times on shift 2_____         Injury likelihood._____
    number of times on shift 3_____         (use letters above)

they are unreliable for small workforces (i.e., exposures below 200,000 man hours for the BLS formula; Tarrants, 1980).

In addition to the injury event rate, data were obtained from personnel records on the types of injury events that had occurred within the previous five-year period. (The injuries that resulted from these recorded events were also collected but were not used in this study.)

*Unreported injury events.* The unreported injury event measure was developed from the content of the injury event records and the near injury event interviews. Respondents were asked to indicate the number of unreported events and resulting injuries that occurred during the past year and the shift the worker was on when each event occurred. Similar to the near events measure, the one-year time span for the unreported events measure was adopted to minimize distortion for these subjective estimates. Open-ended questions about unreported events and injuries not covered in the questionnaire were also included. An example of selected items from the unreported injury events and injuries measure from one organization is provided in Table 2.

## Phase 2: Data Collection

All production workers in both the plastics and glass plants who did not participate in the initial critical incidents interviews were asked to fill out the near injury events and unreported injury events measures, and relevant demographic and validity measures (discussed next).

Participants were asked to identify themselves on the consent forms so their responses could be yoked to recorded events data. The surveys, however, only contained identifying numbers. All participants were assured complete confidentiality.

*Work safety and hazards.* Perceptions of Safety Practices and Programs is a 10-item scale developed from the dimensions of safety climate identified by Zohar (1980). It deals with how much management and the organization care about safety, the adequacy of existing safety training and rules, and whether safe work performance is rewarded. Coefficient alphas for sample 1 = .59; sample 2 = .28. Because the reliability of the safety scale was unacceptably low in sample 2, it was excluded from any further statistical analyses.

Perceptions of Workplace Hazards is a 10-item scale developed from concerns identified in Smith, Cohen, Cohen, and Cleveland (1978). It asks how safe the work environment is perceived to be and the likelihood of injuries. Coefficient alphas for sample 1 = .71; sample 2 = .63.

*Sleep complaints.* A scale used by Torsvall and Åkerstedt (1980) was modified and adapted for this study by adding an additional item

TABLE 2. Selected Items from Unreported Injury Events Questionnaire

Now we would like you to give us information about accidents that happened to you in the past 12 months that you did not report to your supervisor, foreman, or the nurse. Write down your best estimate of the number of times this accident happened (but you did not report it) on each shift (1 = day, 2 = afternoon, and 3 = midnight shifts) and any injuries resulting from these accidents (using the letters from the list of injuries below). If a single accident resulted in several injuries, please write all of the injuries down using the letters below.

ACCIDENTS

**I was struck by equipment or an object.**

number of times on:
Shift 1_____    Injuries resulted_____
Shift 2_____    Injuries resulted_____
Shift 3_____    Injuries resulted_____

**I hit part of my body on something.**

number of times on:
Shift 1_____    Injuries resulted_____
Shift 2_____    Injuries resulted_____
Shift 3_____    Injuries resulted_____

**I slipped on something on the floor.**

number of times on:
Shift 1_____    Injuries resulted_____
Shift 2_____    Injuries resulted_____
Shift 3_____    Injuries resulted_____

**I fell down.**

number of times on:
Shift 1_____    Injuries resulted_____
Shift 2_____    Injuries resulted_____
Shift 3_____    Injuries resulted_____

**I was exposed to a chemical or dust (on skin or in air).**

number of times on:
Shift 1_____    Injuries resulted_____
Shift 2_____    Injuries resulted_____
Shift 3_____    Injuries resulted_____

INJURIES
A = Lacerations/cut
B = Back Strain
C = Pulled Muscle
D = Eye irritation
E = Bruise/swelling
F = Puncture
G = Sore joint/muscle
H = Jammed finger/toe
I = Object in/under skin
J = Rash on skin
K = Burn on skin
L = Burned eye
M = Sick to stomach
N = Problems breathing
O = Sprained ankle
P = Torn muscle/tendon
Q = Concussion
R = Broken bone
S = Hernia
T = Amputation

("Do you wake up frequently during the night?"). This 5-item scale deals with frequencies of various sleep complaints, such as difficulty in falling or staying asleep. Coefficient alphas for sample 1 = .61; sample 2 = .70.

*Morningness.* Personal preference for morning or evening activities (i.e., morning or evening types), a widely acknowledged individual difference in human circadian functioning, was assessed with the 12-item Preferences Scale (Smith et al., 1993). This scale deals with preferences for engaging in routine activities, such as sleeping, working, and exercising, at different times of the 24-hour day. Evening types seem to show more flexibility in their sleeping patterns and are able to alter their sleep-wake cycle (e.g., shiftwork) with less discomfort than morning types (Kerkhof, 1985; Monk & Folkard, 1985). Coefficient alphas for sample 1 = .83; sample 2 = .86.

The above variables were chosen to establish the validity of the injury event measures because the safety, hazards, sleep complaints, and morningness scales have demonstrated relations with industrial injuries or performance in prior research (e.g., see Kerkhof, 1985; Leigh, 1986; Lavie, Kremerman, & Wiel, 1982). Specifically, those shiftworkers who reported a hazardous work environment, poor quality sleep, and difficulty in adapting to schedule changes should also experience more injury events.

The safety, hazards, and sleep complaints scales were adapted by the researchers specifically for studying industrial injury events. All self-report scales developed for this study (including the near and unreported injury events measures) were pilot tested in another (light metal) manufacturing plant and were found to have acceptable measurement properties.

The demographic variables examined here are company and job tenure, age, and hours of overtime.

## *RESULTS AND DISCUSSION*

To assess the validity of the self-reported injury event data, correlations were computed between the injury event measures and demographics, work safety, work hazards, sleep complaints, and morningness (Tables 3 & 4). The frequency rates for each injury event measure were used in statistical analyses. Both parametric and non-parametric measures of association were calculated for these measures. Because few differences existed between the two types of analyses, only the parametric analyses (Pearson correlation coefficients), which should be considered conservative estimates, are reported here.

*Sample 1.* Company tenure correlated positively with recorded injury events ($r = .24$, $p < .01$) and unreported injury events ($r = .28$, $p <$

TABLE 3. Correlations Between Study Variables and Injury Events

Sample 1 (Plastics Plant)

| Variable | Recorded injury events | Unreported injury events | Near injury events |
|---|---|---|---|
| 1. Recorded injury events | | | |
| 2. Unreported injury events | .13 | | |
| 3. Near injury events | .14 | .53*** | |
| 4. Company tenure | .24** | .28** | .13 |
| 5. Job tenure | .23* | .18 | .19$^{†}$ |
| 6. Age | .12 | .01 | −.09 |
| 7. Hours of overtime | .01 | .16 | .21* |
| 8. Safety practices | −.23* | −.17 | −.30*** |
| 9. Hazards | .04 | .20* | .24** |
| 10. Sleep complaints | .21* | .08 | .19* |
| 11. Morningness | .12 | .18$^{†}$ | .07 |

$^{†}$ = .05. *p < .05. **p < .01. ***p < .001
N = 115.

TABLE 4. Correlations Between Study Variables and Injury Events

Sample 2 (Glass Plant)

| Variable | Recorded injury events | Unreported injury events | Near injury events |
|---|---|---|---|
| 1. Recorded injury events | | | |
| 2. Unreported injury events | .03 | | |
| 3. Near injury events | .06 | .60$^{†}$ | |
| 4. Company tenure | −.03 | −.13 | −.02 |
| 5. Job tenure | −.01 | −.11 | −.05 |
| 6. Age | .01 | −.11 | −.20** |
| 7. Hours of overtime | .21** | .03 | .01 |
| 8. Safety practices | --- | --- | --- |
| 9. Hazards | .15 | .23** | .17* |
| 10. Sleep complaints | −.08 | .07 | .02 |
| 11. Morningness | .00 | −.02 | −.03 |

*p < .10. **p < .05. ***p < .01. $^{†}$ = .0001
N = 120.

.01), and job tenure correlated positively with recorded events (r = .23, p < .05) and near events (r = .19, p = .05). Hours of overtime, however, related positively only with near events (r = .21, p < .05). Age did not correlate with any of the event variables. Thus, as expected, the shift-workers with greater company and job tenure, and/or hours of overtime, reported more injury events. This type of result has been reported before (e.g., Hansen, 1989) and simply implies that the more experienced worker is undoubtedly involved in more (and perhaps more difficult) tasks and activities at work. Greater overtime, of course, should also be related to a higher activity level and hence more opportunities for injury events at work.

Perceptions of work hazards correlated positively with unreported injury events ($r = .20$, $p < .05$) and near events ($r = .24$, $p < .01$). Safety practices and programs correlated negatively with recorded events ($r = -.23$, $p < .05$) and near events ($r = -.30$, $p < .001$). Reported sleep complaints related positively to recorded injury events ($r = .21$, $p < .05$) and near events ($r = .19$, $p < .05$), although morningness correlated positively only with unreported injury events ($r = .18$, $p = .05$). These results indicate that, as expected, participants who reported greater work hazards and fewer safety practices also reported increased work injuries. Greater sleep complaints imply that the workers were experiencing poor quality or insufficient sleep, which should increase the likelihood of injuries. Because a more extreme morning orientation suggests that the sleep-wake cycle has advanced, resulting in earlier awakenings, and that sleep has become less flexible (i.e., the hours of sleep are more difficult to alter) (Åkerstedt & Torsvall, 1981; Tepas, Duchon, & Gersten, 1993), shiftworkers with an advanced morning orientation should also experience increased injuries.

The only significant relationship among the three event measures (recorded, unreported, and near) was between near and unreported injury events ($r = .53$, $p < .001$). These correlations (or lack of same) suggest that the three event measures may be different constructs.

*Sample 2.* Age correlated with near injury events ($r = -.20$, $p < .05$), and hours of overtime correlated with recorded events ($r = .21$, $p < .05$). Company and job tenure were not related to any injury event measures. Therefore, participants indicated that, as the worker's age increased, fewer near events were reported and that increased overtime was associated with more recorded events.

Work hazards correlated both with unreported injury events ($r = .23$, $p < .05$) and near events ($r = .17$, $p = .05$). No relationships existed between any injury event and work hazards, sleep complaints, and morningness. (Safety practices, as mentioned previously, were not analyzed in sample 2.)

Similar to plant 1, an association between injury event measures was found only between unreported and near events ($r = .60$, $p < .0001$). This result indicates that the three injury event measures are not redundant, thus suggesting different constructs.

As discussed previously, sample 2 was particularly problematic because of an adversarial relationship between labor and management at the glass plant, as well as other organizational constraints. We believe that these issues probably affected not only the response rate but also the quality of the data obtained. Because these data from sample 2 were more skewed than sample 1, we also investigated non-parametric measures of association (e.g., Kendall's tau and Spearman's rho) and transformation (normalization) procedures. However, regardless of the approach, the results for the glass plant changed very little.

Across both plants (samples), a few common themes emerged. Specifically, the results from both samples showed that an injury event measure (sample 1: near events & sample 2: recorded events) was related to hours of overtime. Also, work hazards correlated with both unreported and near injury events in both plants. Given the differences in the two samples, the take-home message is quite direct: Hours of overtime and perception of work hazards are promising predictors of injury events. These two variables could be used by management or safety departments to monitor the possibility of future injury events and resulting injuries, thus providing an impetus for change. In addition, near and unreported injury events were correlated, although they were not related to recorded events in either plant. These results indicate that the self-report measures of injury events may be measuring something different from recorded injury events. These results are especially promising, given that recorded (file) data are often inadequately documented and organized.

## CONCLUSIONS

This study involved the development of an injury event research protocol using near miss and unreported injury events to assess injury event occurrence in addition to recorded events. These variables provide researchers with data beyond recorded events, which, as discussed previously, are often uncommon and poorly recorded or omitted. As indicated by the results in both plants, unreported and near events are related to variables relevant to injury event occurrence (e.g., work hazards) beyond the few relationships found with recorded events. The self-report event measures, although correlated, demonstrate no association with recorded events.

One may conjecture why the self-reported events in both plants are so interrelated and yet unrelated to recorded data. One rather obvious answer is that the high correlations between the self-report measures may primarily be the result of common method variance (Howard, 1994; Spector, 1994). Although the recorded data may also be self-report, the reporting style is different (i.e., not through employee surveys), and the injury event may be verified by other sources. However, the correlations between the unreported and near miss data are far from unity (i.e., $r = .53$, plant 1; $r = .60$, plant 2). Also, the pattern of correlations between the two self-report measures and work-related variables mostly differ. These data suggest that near misses and unreported events are capturing different aspects of the injury process.

The traditional argument is that recorded or archival data are superior to employee self-reports because recorded data are not as susceptible to response or reporting biases (e.g., the tendency to look good or uninjured). However, the review of research on the weaknesses of recorded data in the introduction indicates otherwise. Given the low associations between the self-reported (unreported and near misses) and recorded data, we must assume that each type is capturing something different in the two data sets, even if all are error-prone in some way. Indeed, although each type of data is related to important work-related variables, the self-report measures are related to different (and largely more) variables than the recorded events.

Therefore, the data that have been collected on these self-report event measures suggest that they may be separate constructs from recorded events and consequently have potential utility as additional injury event measures. As such, they may considerably enhance our understanding of the injury event process, and thereby enable researchers to develop a clearer understanding of the etiology of industrial injury events.

Several limitations of the current study should be noted. First, the near miss and unreported events measures are all self-report, which are subject to a variety of perceptual biases. However, the use of these types of data, particularly near event data, has long been recommended in injury event research (Chapanis, 1959). Second, the samples used in the validity assessment were small, and, therefore, lack of statistical power may have precluded finding a larger number of significant effects. Also, as mentioned earlier, the quality of the data from the second (glass) plant was suspect, which may have biased the results. Third, because the unreported and near event measures were developed from data specific to manufacturing plants, they are not generalizable outside the industry for which they were developed. Information about near and unreported events, however, is usually easily obtainable within the context of safety research or programs.

One final limitation is that data collection for the self-report event measures covered a very limited time span (one year). Recorded event rates would, within a one-year span, usually be quite limited, although a comparison of these data with five years of recorded event data from the same plant produced no notable differences. The limited time span for the near and unreported event data was deemed necessary because these data are retrospective self-reports and therefore subject to distortions from memory. However, in reality, organizational records are often poorly documented or not documented at all. Limited time spans for data collection and multiple injury event measures may indeed be the only viable options for the safety researcher in many industrial settings.

In sum, across two manufacturing organizations, we demonstrated that self-report injury event measures are independent from typical recorded event measures and are related to accepted work injury-relevant variables (e.g., work hazards, hours of overtime). An expanded protocol incorporating both self-report and recorded event data may provide future safety researchers and practitioners with additional tools to investigate the injury event process.

## REFERENCES

Åkerstedt, T., & Torsvall, L. (1981). Shift dependent well-being and individual differences. *Ergonomics, 24*, 265-273.

Chapanis, A. (1959). *Research techniques in human engineering.* Baltimore: The John Hopkins Press.

Fingar, A. R., Hopkins, R. S., & Nelson, M. (1992). Work-related injuries in Athens County, 1982 to 1986: A comparison of emergency department and workers' compensation data, *Journal of Occupational Medicine, 34*, 779-787.

Flanagan, J. C. (1954). The critical incident technique. *Psychological Bulletin, 51*, 327-358.

Hansen, C. P. (1989). A causal model of the relationship among accidents, biodata, personality, and cognitive factors. *Journal of Applied Psychology, 74*(1), 81-90.

Howard, G. S. (1994). Why do people say nasty things about self-reports? *Journal of Organizational Behavior, 15*, 399-404.

Kerkhof, G. (1985). Inter-individual differences in the human circadian system: A review. *Biological Psychology, 20*, 83-112.

Lavie, P., Kremerman, S., & Wiel, M. (1982). Sleep disorders and safety in industrial workers. *Accident Analysis and Prevention, 14*, 311-314.

Leigh, J. (1986). Individual and job characteristics as predictors of industrial accidents. *Accident Analysis and Prevention, 18*, 209-216.

Levin, L., Oler, J., & Whiteside, J. (1985). Injury incidence rates in a paint production company on rotating production shifts. *Accident Analysis and Prevention, 17*, 67-73.

Monk, T., & Folkard, S. (1985). Shiftwork and performance. In S. Folkard & T. Monk (Eds.), *Hours of work: Temporal factors in work-scheduling*. Chichester: John Wiley & Sons.

Murphy, P. L., Sorock, G. S., Courtney, T. K., Webster, B. S., & Leamon, T. B. (1996). Injury and illness in the American workplace: A comparison of data sources. *American Journal of Industrial Medicine, 30*, 130-141.

Oleinick, A., Guire, K. E., Hawthorne, V. M., Shock, M. A., Sluck, J. V., Lee, B., & La, S. (1993). Current methods for estimating severity for occupational injuries and illnesses: Data from the 1986 Michigan comprehensive compensable injury and illness database. *American Journal of Industrial Medicine, 23*, 231-252.

Pransky, G., Snyder, T., Dembe, A., & Himmelstein, J. (1999). Under-reporting of work-related disorders in the workplace: A case study and review of the literature. *Ergonomics, 42*(1), 171-182.

Seligman, P. J., Sieber, W. K., Pederson, D. H., Sundin, D. S., & Frazier, T. M. (1988). Compliance with OSHA record-keeping requirements. *American Journal of Public Health, 78*(9), 1218-1219.

Smith, C. S., Folkard, S., Schmeider, R. A., Parra, L. F., Spelten, E., & Almirall, H. (1998). An exploratory investigation of morning-evening orientation in six countries using a new measure of morningness. Manuscript submitted for publication.

Smith, C. S., Silverman, G. S., Heckert, T. M., Brodke, M. H., Hayes, B. E., Silverman, M. K., & Mattimore, L. K. (1997). Shift-related differences in industrial injuries: Application of a new research method in fixed-shift and rotating-shift systems. *International Journal of Occupational and Environmental Health, 3*, Supplement 2, S46-S52.

Smith, M., Cohen, H., Cohen, A., & Cleveland, R. (1978). Characteristics of successful safety programs. *Journal of Safety Research, 10*, 5-15.

Spector, P. E. (1994). Using self-report questionnaires in OB research: A comment on the use of a controversial method. *Journal of Organizational Behavior, 15*, 285-392.

Tarrants, W. (1980). *The measurement of safety performance*. New York: Garland, STPM Press.

Tepas, D.I., Duchon, J.C., & Gersten, A.H. (1993). Shiftwork and the older worker. *Experimental Aging Research, 19*, 295-320.

Torsvall, L., & Åkerstedt, T. (1980). A diurnal type scale. *Scandinavian Journal of Work and Environmental Health, 6*, 283-290.

Weddle, M. G. (1996). Reporting occupational injuries: The first step. *Journal of Safety Research, 27*(4), 217-223.

Wojtczak-Jaroszowa, J., & Jarosz, D. (1987). Time-related distribution of occupational accidents. *Journal of Safety Research, 18*, 33-41.

Zohar, D. (1980). Safety climate in industrial organizations: Theoretical and applied implications. *Journal of Applied Psychology, 65*, 96-102.

# Gender Issues in the Measurement
# of Physical and Psychological Safety

Dennis Doverspike
Alana Blumental

University of Akron

**SUMMARY.** Traditional methods of analyzing the physical and psychological demands of the job have been criticized as potentially biased against female sex-typed jobs. This poses a potential problem when information about the job is used to develop safety training programs or injury prevention programs. In this paper, the problem of measuring safety-related aspects of jobs is explored from a perspective which incorporates attention to gender issues. Potential problems are identified in the measurement of characteristics such as physical safety, responsibility for the physical safety of others, and psychological safety. A shortcoming in the literature deserving of further research is also identified in terms of the relative paucity of measures of responsibility for psychological safety. The failure to pay attention to gender issues may lead to problems in safety training, due to deficiencies in assessment, evaluation, and design. *[Article copies available for a fee from The Haworth Document Delivery Service: 1-800-342-9678. E-mail address: <getinfo@haworthpressinc.com> Website: <http://www.HaworthPress.com> © 2001 by The Haworth Press, Inc. All rights reserved.]*

**KEYWORDS.** Gender issues, psychological safety, physical safety, safety, safety training

Address correspondence to: Dennis Doverspike, Psychology Department, University of Akron, Akron, OH 44325-4301 (E-mail: ddoverspike@uakron.edu).

The authors would like to acknowledge the helpful comments provided by Jan Yoder, PhD, and Linda Karbonet, MD.

[Haworth co-indexing entry note]: "Gender Issues in the Measurement of Physical and Psychological Safety." Doverspike, Dennis, and Alana Blumental. Co-published simultaneously in *Journal of Prevention & Intervention in the Community* (The Haworth Press, Inc.) Vol. 22, No. 1, 2001, pp. 21-34; and: *Workplace Safety: Individual Differences in Behavior* (ed: Alice F. Stuhlmacher, and Douglas F. Cellar) The Haworth Press, Inc., 2001, pp. 21-34. Single or multiple copies of this article are available for a fee from The Haworth Document Delivery Service [1-800-342-9678, 9:00 a.m. - 5:00 p.m. (EST). E-mail address: getinfo@haworthpress inc.com].

The purpose of this paper is to explore the problem of measuring safety-related aspects of jobs from a perspective which incorporates attention to gender issues. While on the surface, safety might appear to be a topic free of gender concerns, feminist scholars (Dumais, 1992; Messing, 1992, 1997, 1998) have argued that health and safety issues, in general, are often approached from a masculine viewpoint. Such a viewpoint tends to be centered upon male health or safety issues and traditionally male dominated occupations. Hereinafter, we will use the terms male or female sex-typed jobs to refer to occupations traditionally viewed as dominated by males or females, respectively; this reflects normal usage of the term in the field and is not meant to dismiss the importance of individual differences nor the problems encountered by men and women in nontraditional occupations.

This gender bias argument can take several forms. First, safety research has customarily been directed at male sex-typed jobs such as those in mining and manufacturing. Second, research on safety issues has often excluded or minimized the participation of women. For example, a recent article by Hofmann and Stetzer (1998) on safety included two studies where the participants were 96% male and 93% male, respectively. Third, unique aspects of women's health issues, such as safety topics related to reproductive problems, have been ignored (Dumais, 1992; Messing, 1992, 1997, 1998).

Even if we do not accept the gender bias argument in total, one can understand how the argument can be made that workplace safety has often been more concerned with jobs, occupations, and industries which are dominated by men. Therefore, a consideration of gender issues can broaden our vistas in addressing the issues of safety and accident prevention. In addition, by considering the topic of gender, we are also led to a broader view of the dimensions of safety, one which considers not only physical safety but the increased importance of psychological safety.

In this paper, the perspective taken is one derived from job analysis, sometimes also referred to as task analysis, and the traditions of the field of Industrial/Organizational Psychology. In taking this viewpoint, we do not intend to slight the insights offered by other approaches such as Industrial Sociology, Feminist Psychology, or Human Factors and Ergonomics. Each of these alternative disciplines has much to offer, and at times we borrow from the insights gleaned from other fields. However, the Industrial/Organizational Psychology perspective is important because of the impact the job analysis process has on human resource management practices, in general, including selection, training, compensation decisions, and, of course, safety issues including training and climate assessments.

For the field of Industrial/Organizational Psychology, the two major safety-related issues have been: (1) how do we measure the tasks or activities on the job and/or the worker requirements/abilities which are related to safety; and (2) how do we develop effective accident prevention or safety interventions. Within the job analysis arena, the major question has been how do we best measure the tasks, duties, functions, and responsibilities of the job related to safety and how do we turn these measurements into statements regarding worker requirements. It is this issue of measurement, and gender issues in this measurement, which is of particular interest in this paper. Our assumption, which we believe a fundamental assumption of the training field, is that the rational design of safety training programs and prevention efforts begin with adequate measurement. If our measurement is biased based upon gender, then our training programs will reflect this bias. Although our major concern is with the area of measurement and job analysis, we also do then comment on applications to effective safety prevention interventions.

## THE MEASUREMENT OF SAFETY-RELATED ASPECTS OF THE JOB

Measures of safety-related aspects of the job are usually completed as part of an overall analysis of the job, the task or job analysis. This analysis of the job provides detailed information on the tasks or functions required to be completed in order to perform the job proficiently. It also provides information on worker requirements, often referred to as KSAs, or knowledge, skills, and abilities, required in order to perform the job (McCormick, 1979). Job analysis information may be acquired by observation, questionnaire, or interview. The information may be supplied by a specially trained observer, a job incumbent, or a supervisor. Today, it is quite common to use some type of structured or semi-structured questionnaire which may be completed by the incumbent and the supervisor. Over time, various standardized questionnaires have been developed. Although many of these questionnaires are proprietary, some are published and widely available (McCormick,

1979). A review of these questionnaires suggests that they tend to tap the same basic factors and ask the same basic questions about safety issues.

The three major factors or dimensions of safety usually measured include physical safety, working conditions, and responsibility for the physical safety of others. Responses to the physical safety and working conditions factors are usually very highly correlated such that jobs which receive high ratings on one dimension receive high ratings on the other and they seem to be part of the same major factor. Therefore, we have discussed threats to one's own physical safety and working conditions under the same heading. Examples of a typical physical safety scale and responsibility for the physical safety of others scale appear in Tables 1 and 2 (The examples in Tables 1 through 3 are adapted from Doverspike, 1983; the scales presented there have been abbreviated here due to space considerations).

Corresponding to the scales or major dimensions, there are individual questions or survey items. These questions correspond to the individual statements contained in the scales presented in Tables 1 and 2. For example, common questions for physical safety and responsibility for physical safety are listed in Tables 1 and 2 respectively.

Psychological safety is not often treated as a separate dimension, but is contained in or measured by Mental Effort or Stress scales. This

TABLE 1. Prototypical Measure of Physical Safety

Definition: This factor measures the degree to which the job requires unusual physical effort or exertion and the hazards associated with the job.

Levels:
1   Limited. The work is sedentary and requires normal physical exertion. The work may require occasional walking, standing, bending, driving of an automobile, or carrying of materials weighing less than 5 pounds. Involves excellent working conditions with limited probability of injury.

2   Moderate. Requires moderate physical effort. The work involves frequently working with material weighing 5-25 pounds or periodically working with material weighing 25-50 pounds. Involves exposure to injuries which may result in loss of fingers or toes or broken bones.

3   Considerable. Requires considerable to heavy physical effort. The work involves working consistently with material weighing 25-50 pounds or frequently with material weighing over 50 pounds. Involves exposure to injuries which may result in permanent disability or death.

Typical Questions:
   How often do you have to climb a ladder?
   How often do you have to chase someone more than 100 yards?
   What is the probability of an injury involving total disability?

TABLE 2. Prototypical Measure of Responsibility for Physical Safety

Definition: This factor measures the degree to which the job requires responsibility for the safety of others and to which errors may lead to injury to others.

Level:
1 Little or No Responsibility. Requires little or no responsibility for the physical safety of others, who are generally able to protect themselves from injury. Errors will not normally result in injury to others.

2 Reasonable Attention. Requires reasonable attention and responsibility to safeguard against the occurrence or circumstances of action which create dangerous situations for others. Applies to many situations where there is a possibility of injury, but constant attention is not required.

3 Maximum Responsibility. Requires constant attention and responsibility to safeguard against the occurrence of actions or circumstances which create dangerous situations for others. Victims of actions or fellow workers can do relatively little to prevent injury.

Typical Questions:
If the employee made a mistake, what is the likelihood that someone else would experience an injury such as a broken bone?
How often does the employee have to pay constant attention in order to ensure that the employee's actions do not endanger the physical safety of others?
If the employee made a mistake, what is the likelihood it would lead to someone else experiencing an injury such as a cut, bruise or burn?

TABLE 3. Prototypical Measure of Mental Effort

Definition: This factor measures the degree to which the position requires unusual mental effort, mental strain, or mental stress due to workload, deadlines or the strain of interpersonal relationships.

Level:
1 None. Requires no special mental effort.
2 Some. Requires occasional deadlines. Requires occasional phone or personal contact with others who may become verbally abusive.
3 Extreme. Requires constant concentration to a very large volume of work. Job is such that a feeling of mental pressure exists. Requires constant overtime.

Typical Questions:
How often do you have conflicting deadlines?
How often do you have to negotiate with others who are resistant to your arguments?
How often do you deal with the public?

would appear to be a weakness in the job analysis literature. With the increased presence of human and social service jobs (e.g., childcare worker, police officer, social worker) in our economy, psychological safety would appear to be becoming as important a factor as physical safety. An example of this type of scale, a Mental Effort scale, appears in Table 3. Typically, responsibility for the psychological safety of others has not been measured, although we would argue it should be. Again, the shift to service jobs in our economy would seem to lead to an increased need to assess responsibility for psychological safety. Due to the general lack of measures of this type, we have not attempted to provide an example of a typical scale.

## GENDER ISSUES IN THE MEASUREMENT OF SAFETY-RELATED ASPECTS OF THE JOB

Traditional job analysis and the associated questionnaires and scales for measuring safety have been criticized by a variety of social critics based on speculation that a number of work-related activities are performed more often by women than by men and that these gender-related activities are often not evaluated by standard, structured questionnaires. Basically, this argument usually takes the form that female sex-typed jobs tend to have different and specific characteristics, for example, repetition and monotony, which differ from the critical safety-related characteristics of male sex-typed jobs. Then, as a result of most safety and health studies focusing on male sex-typed jobs, the characteristics of female sex-typed jobs relevant to safety issues and health tend to be ignored in assessments and interventions.

The discussion of possible gender issues in job analysis has centered on both the typical question level, whether an item, a statement, or an indicator, and the major characteristic or scale level. Most of the discussion of specific problems with items or statements parallels the discussion of problems with major characteristics. Based on a comprehensive review conducted by the authors of the research relevant to gender issues, we believe that the literature can be appropriately divided into concerns with the measurement of physical safety and the argument that psychological safety issues are often ignored.

### Physical Safety

Research in the area of gender issues in job analysis has identified physical safety as a major area in which there appears to be problems in measurement for female sex-typed jobs. Using traditional measures of physical safety, there is typically about a half to a whole standard deviation difference between the mean scores for male and female sex-typed jobs on scales, with the female mean being very close to the scale floor or lowest possible level (Doverspike & Barrett, 1984; Doverspike & Barrett, 1999). However, critics of traditional measures argue that as a result of the unique nature of the physical requirements of female sex-typed jobs, current scales do not provide an adequate assessment of physical safety (Kessler-Harris, 1988; Remick, 1984; Steinberg, 1990; VanderBurg & Schoemaker, 1985).

Female sex-typed jobs are more likely than male sex-typed jobs to be characterized by precise movements which are seen as failing to capture the precise movements, constrained and restricted movement, use of fine motor skills, attention to detail, repetition, and the performance of monotonous work which typify female sex-typed jobs (Doverspike & Barrett, 1984; Kessler-Harris, 1988; Remick, 1984; Steinberg, 1990; VanderBurg & Schoemaker, 1985). The characteristics of female sex-typed jobs are seen as having the potential to lead to physical effects such as circulatory problems, eye strain, mental and physical fatigue, strained muscles, musculoskeletal problems, allergies and skin diseases as opposed to the broken bones or lost limbs likely to characterize injuries in male sex-typed jobs (Eyde, 1983; Messing, 1998). In addition, women may experience health and safety problems related to reproductive functions (Messing, 1998). In terms of specific environmental factors, female sex-typed jobs are more likely to be characterized by exposure to cleaning agents and harsh chemicals, noises from office equipment, and exposure to the health problems of other people (Eyde, 1983; Messing, 1998; Steinberg & Haignere, 1987).

Recently, the repetitive movement characteristics of many female sex-typed jobs have also been linked to a variety of disorders including repetitive strain injuries (RSI), although the exact nature of these links is still a controversial topic. RSI symptoms include a variety of painful or debilitating conditions which are thought to be caused by repetitive hand or arm movement. RSI complaints in Australia were found to be predominantly reported by women who performed extensive typing activities (Kiesler & Finholt, 1988).

While traditionally female sex-typed jobs may not be immediately thought of as requiring a great deal of lifting, many service occupations, nursing for example, require repetitive lifting operations. While the type of lifting required in these service jobs may require the movement of objects, people, or items which are quite heavy, it more typically involves the repeated lifting of lighter objects. This type of repetitive lifting can be found on many female sex-typed jobs and can lead to muscular fatigue and musculoskeletal disorders. Thus, traditional approaches which simply assess the maximum amount lifted may fail to capture the continuous lifting demands which are held to be characteristic of female sex-typed jobs.

## *Responsibility for the Physical Safety of Others*

The responsibility for the physical safety of others has often been conceptualized in terms of prototypical male sex-typed jobs such as bus driver or airline pilot. Using traditional measures of responsibility for the physical safety of others, there is typically about a half to a whole standard deviation difference between the mean scores for male and female sex-typed jobs on scales, with the female mean being very close to the scale floor or lowest possible level (Doverspike & Barrett, 1984; Doverspike & Barrett, 1999). However, the critics of traditional measures argue that female sex-typed jobs do involve responsibility for the physical safety of others or for so-called "life-and-death" issues (Major & Konar, 1984). Examples of female sex-typed jobs which involve substantial responsibility for the physical safety of others include such obvious choices as nurses, dental assistants, and some social workers. Less obvious examples of jobs with responsibility for the physical safety of others include occupations such as food service employees, hair styling work, and even janitorial positions.

## *Psychological Safety*

Psychological safety is a major factor or characteristic of work which has been found to be associated more often with jobs performed predominantly by women. This would include both responsibility for the psychological well-being of others and also threats to one's own psychological safety. Often on traditional questionnaires, an indirect attempt is made to measure the threat a job poses to one's own psychological safety. This is commonly accomplished through scales labeled as measuring mental effort or stress. Often, however, these scales may not measure aspects of mental effort relevant to female sex-typed jobs. Specific characteristics related to mental effort or psychological safety which appear to be more characteristic of female sex-typed jobs include the ability to handle role conflicts such as continually changing demands, managing multiple roles, and handling the duties of multiple positions (Barnett, Marshall, & Singer, 1992; Basow, 1986). Role conflict may be especially prevalent in secretarial and clerical jobs. Failure to manage this role conflict can lead to both psychological and physical distress. As compared to men, women appear to be at greater risk to experience psychological and psychophysiological stress disorders and also to experience depression (Collins et al., 1997).

One problem with attempting to measure psychological safety through stress is that what is stressful is frequently subject to individual interpretation. That is, the same job function or task which is boring to one individual may seem quite demanding to the next person. As a result, it is often difficult to measure mental effort as a property of the job independent of the subjective experience of stress.

The same basic issue applies in trying to measure monotony, which, depending upon one's viewpoint, could be seen as the opposite of mental effort. Monotony is often difficult to measure reliably since the interpretation of the same characteristic may vary widely across individuals. Again, what one person finds monotonous, another person may find to be a challenge. Previous attempts to measure monotony have also run into difficulties with monotony being negatively correlated with almost all other important job factors.

## *Responsibility for the Psychological Safety of Others*

In addition to threats to psychological safety, female sex-typed jobs are more likely to involve responsibility for the psychological safety of others including responsibility for emotional well-being, ethical responsibility, and social responsibility (Major & Konar, 1984). Female sex-typed jobs are also more likely to involve responsibility for the development of others, providing for the needs of others, and sensitivity to others' psychological states (Kessler-Harris, 1988). Jobs of this type include social worker, crisis counselors, and teachers. Some examples of behaviors which impact on psychological safety include: (1) performing employee or client counseling involving diagnosis, development of strategies, remedial work, or career guidance; (2) teaching courses involving intensive work with students or clients; (3) providing emotional assistance in the form of rehabilitative services. Errors in the performance of these behaviors can result in minor or major psychological or emotional problems depending upon the client population. In addition, in administrative positions, errors, inappropriate decisions or inappropriate recommendations can lead to widespread losses in public confidence, major health or public welfare issues, failures to meet the requirements of regulatory agencies, or failures to meet critical deadlines (e.g., loss of a major federal grant for child development programs due to a failure to submit a proposal in time).

Unfortunately, very few traditional job analysis instruments appear to tap this dimension of responsibility for psychological safety. It is much more common to find the assessment of characteristics associated with male sex-typed jobs, such as financial responsibility, supervisory responsibility, or responsibility for the physical safety of others, than it is to find measures of responsibility for psychological safety. For this reason, we have not included an example of a traditional scale measuring this construct, as responsibility for psychological safety itself appears to be a nontraditional job dimension. We would argue that this is a serious oversight and that research attention should be directed toward developing adequate measures of responsibility for psychological safety.

## CONCLUSIONS AND IMPLICATIONS
## FOR SAFETY TRAINING AND PREVENTION

The development of effective safety training and prevention programs depends upon the existence of appropriate techniques for assessment and evaluation. In order to accurately assess and evaluate the effectiveness of safety training and prevention programs, reliable, valid, and bias-free measures of important job characteristics related to safety are needed. Within the job analysis tradition, safety has most frequently been measured in terms of aspects of physical safety, including threats to one's own physical safety and responsibility for the physical safety of others. Critics of traditional job analysis have argued that the currently available methods for assessing jobs fail to adequately measure the important characteristics of female sex-typed jobs. Although this question can be assessed empirically (c.f., Doverspike & Barrett, 1984), a rational analysis of the available literature suggests that there may, in fact, be deficiencies related to gender in current job analysis-based measures of safety.

In order to develop more gender-balanced measures of physical safety, it would appear to be appropriate to include questions or indicators assessing factors such as the total amount lifted over the course of the day, rather than just the maximum, the amount of dexterity and fine motor control required, the amount of visual strain required, and the necessity to work in small or confined places or sit in unusual and uncomfortable positions. Note that the examples presented here are not intended to be all-inclusive, but are merely offered as examples of some alternatives. Another area of critical importance in the workplace today, which has been underemphasized in the past, is exposure to contagious or fatal diseases. This exposure exists not only in jobs such as nursing, but also in a variety of technical or therapeutic professions where fluids are handled or there is repeated contact with potential carriers of diseases (Collins et al., 1997).

For responsibility for the physical safety of others, it would appear to be appropriate to include questions or indicators assessing factors such as identifying problems (e.g., health-related, service delivery needs, etc.), making referrals and treatment plans, and monitoring progress in order to assist and/or protect others whose physical well-being (e.g., possible injury, health, food, shelter, medical) might otherwise be jeopardized. The definition of physical safety might also be expanded to include physical growth and development.

Currently, psychological safety is frequently assessed indirectly through measures of mental effort or stress. These measures have problems associated with them related to individual differences in reactions to and assessments of stress. It would seem that a better, more representative measure of psychological safety could be developed. In particular, psychological safety could be measured in a more direct fashion similar to measures of physical safety. The development of better measures of psychological safety would seem to represent a sizable challenge to safety researchers.

In addition, safety training programs should be developed to address not only physical safety, but also psychological safety. The typical safety training program often seems to be directed at problems such as lockout, how to use a ladder, or the correct uses of safety equipment. While these are certainly important issues, the growth of the service, health, and human services sector would appear to support a movement toward a greater concern with aspects of psychological safety. Clerical occupations are not immune to psychological disorders. Technological changes such as increased use of computers and video display terminals have been found to lead to not only increased physical symptoms, but also increased psychological problems (Collins et al., 1997; National Research Council, 1983). Technical changes in clerical work can lead to changes in the social climate of work, including supervisory monitoring, which can also lead to an increase in psychological problems (National Research Council, 1983).

Responsibility for the psychological safety of others is an area that has been virtually ignored and therefore is clearly in need of the development of adequate measures. A first step would be to develop measures of responsibility for the psychological safety of others which parallel measures for physical safety. The definition of the psychological health or safety of others could be expanded to include emotional well-being, social development, and mental growth.

In order to avoid problems, the best advice is that safety professionals and those involved in developing safety programs should be cognizant of and sensitive to potential gender biases and gender issues. This would include not only gender bias in the development of training programs, but also gender bias in needs assessment, job analysis, and training evaluation. Safety researchers should design studies which include female participants and persons in female sex-typed jobs, as well as addressing research issues related to health and safety problems relevant to females.

Those interested in safety issues should also be aware of related, relevant topics such as the role of general health promotion (Collins et al., 1997), options in health insurance and benefits, fetal rights and reproductive hazards (Collins et al., 1997; Gonen, 1993), the effects of sexual harassment (Collins et al., 1997), and the effects of apparent safety initiatives on equal employment opportunities for women (Messing, 1998). In addition, while we have concentrated on the job level, careful attention should be paid to the role of individual differences among both men and women in their adaptation to work environments. Finally, one would certainly hope that attempts to improve the occupational safety climate for workers would not lead to the exclusion of classes of workers from desirable jobs and occupations (Collins et al., 1997; Gonen, 1993).

# REFERENCES

Barnett, R. C., Marshall, N. L., & Singer, J. D. (1992). Job experiences over time, multiple roles, and women's mental health: A longitudinal study. *Journal of Personality and Social Psychology, 62,* 634-644.

Basow, S. A. (1986). *Gender stereotypes: Traditions and alternatives* (2nd ed.). Belmont, CA: Brooks/Cole Publishing.

Collins, B. S., Hollander, R. B., Koffman, D. M., Reeve, R., & Seidler, S. (1997). Women, work, and health: Issues and implications for worksite health promotion. *Women & Health, 25,* 3-38.

Doverspike, D. (1983). A statistical analysis of internal sex bias in a job evaluation instrument. *Dissertation Abstracts International, 43,* 3063B.

Doverspike, D., & Barrett, G. V. (1984). An internal bias analysis of a job evaluation instrument. *Journal of Applied Psychology, 69,* 648-662.

Doverspike, D., & Barrett, G. V. (1999). *Investigating differential scale functioning in job evaluation instruments.* Unpublished manuscript, University of Akron, Akron, OH.

Dumais, L. (1992). Impact of the participation of women in science: On rethinking the place of women especially in occupational health. *Women & Health, 18,* 11-25.

Eyde, L. D. (1983). Evaluating job evaluation: Emerging research issues for comparable worth analysis. *Public Personnel Management, 12,* 425-444.

Gonen, J. S. (1993). Women's rights vs. "fetal rights": Politics, law and reproductive hazards in the workplace. *Women & Politics, 13,* 175-190.

Hofmann, D. A., & Stetzer, A. (1998). The role of safety climate and communication in accident interpretation: Implications for learning from negative events. *Academy of Management Journal, 41,* 644-657.

Kessler-Harris, A. (1988). The just price, the free market, and the value of women. *Feminist Studies, 14,* 235-250.

Kiesler, S., & Finholt, T. (1988). The mystery of RSI. *American Psychologist, 43,* 1004-1015.

Major, B., & Konar, E. (1984). An investigation of sex differences in pay expectations and their possible causes. *Academy of Management Journal, 27*(4), 777-792.

McCormick, E. J. (1979). *Job analysis.* New York: AMACOM.

Messing, K. (1992). Introduction: Research directed to improving women's occupational health. *Women & Health, 18,* 1-9.

Messing, K. (1997). Women's occupational health: A critical review and discussion of current issues. *Women & Health, 25,* 39-68.

Messing, K. (1998). Women workers. In R. Wallace, MD, Msc (Ed.), *Public Health and Preventive Medicine* (pp. 693-696). Stamford, CN: Appleton & Lange.

National Research Council (1986). *Computer chips and paper clips: Technology and women's employment.* Washington, DC: National Academy Press.

Remick, H. (1981). The comparable worth controversy. *Public Personnel Management Journal, 10,* 371-383.

Steinberg, R. J. (1990). Social construction of skill: Gender, power, and comparable worth. *Work and Occupations, 17,* 449-482.

Steinberg, R. J., & Haignere, L. (1987). Equitable compensation: Methodological criteria for comparable worth. In C. Bose & G. Spitze (Eds.), *Ingredients for Women's Employment Policy* (pp. 157-182). Albany, NY: State University of New York Press.

VanderBurg, R., & Schoemaker, N. (1985). Scoring women on their labor chances. *Women's Studies International Forum, 8,* 273-278.

# Predicting Motor Vehicle Crash Involvement from a Personality Measure and a Driving Knowledge Test

Winfred Arthur, Jr.

Texas A&M University

Dennis Doverspike

University of Akron

**SUMMARY.** Typically, safety-related driver education programs are aimed at changing knowledge of vehicle operation rules and regulations. However, vehicle crashes are as likely to be related to driver personality variables as they are to the knowledge of vehicle operation and rules and regulations. In a study with 48 licensed drivers, crashes were found to be significantly correlated with conscientiousness, a five-factor model personality dimension, but not with scores on a driving knowledge test. It would appear that prevention efforts should also be directed at changing conscientiousness-related behaviors, including an emphasis on goal-setting, and following rules and regulations. *[Article copies available for a fee from The Haworth Document Delivery Service: 1-800-342-9678. E-mail address: <getinfo@haworthpressinc.com> Website: <http://www.HaworthPress.com> © 2001 by The Haworth Press, Inc. All rights reserved.]*

**KEYWORDS.** Accident prevention, crash prevention, driving behavior, human factors, personality testing, safety behavior

---

Address correspondence to: Winfred Arthur, Jr., Department of Psychology, Texas A&M University, College Station, TX 77843-4235 (E-mail address: wea@psyc.tamu.edu).

[Haworth co-indexing entry note]: "Predicting Motor Vehicle Crash Involvement from a Personality Measure and a Driving Knowledge Test." Arthur, Winfred, and Dennis Doverspike. Co-published simultaneously in *Journal of Prevention & Intervention in the Community* (The Haworth Press, Inc.) Vol. 22, No. 1, 2001, pp. 35-42; and: *Workplace Safety: Individual Differences in Behavior* (ed: Alice F. Stuhlmacher, and Douglas F. Cellar) The Haworth Press, Inc., 2001, pp. 35-42. Single or multiple copies of this article are available for a fee from The Haworth Document Delivery Service [1-800-342-9678, 9:00 a.m. - 5:00 p.m. (EST). E-mail address: getinfo@haworthpressinc.com].

Efforts at preventing vehicle crashes typically focus on driver education efforts. Consequently, driver education receives wide support as one means by which safety on the road can be improved. This implies that a driver's knowledge of vehicular operation principles, and relevant laws and regulations, plays a major role in predicting crashes. Thus, driver education programs are designed to improve driving knowledge and subsequently reduce crash involvement. However, empirical support for the intended effects of driving knowledge on crash involvement is equivocal (Hill & Jamieson, 1978; McKnight & Edwards, 1982; Struckman-Johnson, Lund, Williams, & Osborne, 1989). For example, it has been shown that the use of a motorcycle skill and knowledge test was associated with a 16% reduction in crashes (Anderson, 1980). Jonah, Dawson, and Bragg's (1981) bivariate correlations also showed that high scorers on the Motorcycle Operators Skill Test were more likely to have had an accident than low scorers after a 1-year to 1 1/2-year follow-up. However, their multivariate analysis of variance revealed no effect of test performance on accident involvement. Furthermore, other research has shown that written driver's license tests have very little validity in predicting motor vehicle crashes (Creech & Grandy, 1974; Dreyer, 1976; Kaestner, 1964). Similarly, Hill and Jamieson's (1978) results showed that although a defensive driving course group showed a greater reduction in serious and crash-promoting convictions, they did not show a greater reduction in crashes.

The belief in the efficacy and use of knowledge tests is consistent with the well-established relationship between knowledge and performance, specifically, job performance (Hunter, 1986). However, the specific relationship between driving knowledge and crash involvement may be more tenuous because crash involvement is as much influenced by attitudinal and volition factors as it is by knowledge and ability variables (Parker, Reason, Manstead, & Stradling, 1995; Reason, 1990; Reason, Manstead, Stradling, Baxter, & Campbell, 1990). Consequently, a case could be made that better prediction would be achieved if we take both knowledge and personality/attitudinal variables into account.

Historically, the evidence for systematic links between personality variables and motor vehicle crash involvement has been relatively poor (Arthur, Barrett, & Alexander, 1991). However, unlike the use of variables in other predictor categories (e.g., information processing), research on personality variables has been characterized by a lack of theory and the use of unstandardized, ad hoc questionnaires, inventories, and tests. With the advent of the five-factor model (FFM) of personality (Goldberg, 1993; McCrae & Costa, 1987), there has been a more systematic and comprehensive approach to the study of personality and its relation to overt behaviors. Thus, stronger relationships have been demonstrated between five-factor model personality variables and motor vehicle crash involvement (Arthur & Graziano, 1996).

Until Arthur and Graziano (1996), the relations among the dimensions of the five-factor model and motor vehicle crash involvement had yet to be investigated. This oversight was especially conspicuous, in that personality variables had played a major role in research on vehicular crashes (e.g., Elander, West, & French, 1993). Using two FFM measures in two independent samples, Arthur and Graziano (1996) demonstrated a significant inverse relation between conscientiousness and crash involvement. Individuals who rated themselves as more self-disciplined, responsible, reliable and dependable were less likely to be involved in motor vehicle crashes than those who rated themselves lower on these attributes. The findings were consistent with the premise that highly conscientious individuals are responsive to social obligation norms (Hogan, 1983); they are people who report that they comply with the constraint of laws and public regulations, may engage in less risk-taking, and may avoid dangerous situations (cf., Tomlinson-Keasey & Little, 1990).

Because no single study can provide the definite final statement on the relationship between any two variables, the present study sought to replicate Arthur and Graziano's (1996) conscientiousness/crashes findings. We also extended their work by using a different measure of conscientiousness and also assessed the comparative validity of emotional stability, and a driving knowledge test.

We sought to investigate emotional stability as the second FFM personality variable because one would expect drivers who are more emotionally stable to be less likely to be involved in crashes (Hansen, 1989). A relationship between emotional stability and crashes would be especially likely if we define emotional stability in terms of the subdimensions of attention and distractibility (Hansen, 1989). Auditory selective attention, visual selective attention, and distractibility have all been found to be related to accidents and/or crashes (Arthur et al., 1991; Arthur, Strong, & Williamson, 1994; Hansen, 1989). However, for a more general extroversion factor, the evidence would appear to be inconclusive (Arthur & Graziano, 1996).

## METHOD

### Participants

The participants were 48 volunteers, 16 males and 32 females, from a large, Midwestern University. All 48 were licensed drivers. The average age was 23.96 years ($SD = 8.65$). The average age at which they had started driving was 16.31 ($SD = 1.60$).

### Driving Knowledge Test

The Driving Knowledge Test was a 50-item, multiple choice exam. It was modeled after, but not identical to, the Ohio state driving examination (Ohio Department of Public Safety, 1998). Each question consisted of a stem followed by three alternatives, only one of which was the correct answer. All items were based on the state driving manual. The total score was the number of items answered correctly.

### Conscientiousness Measure

The conscientiousness measure was taken from a standardized personality test used by a major consulting firm. This test was designed to measure the five-factor personality variables. Conscientiousness was measured in terms of four subfactors: goal-setting, following rules, detail-oriented, and order. There were 47 items. Each item consisted of an item stem followed by a 5-step Likert scale ranging from Strongly Disagree to Strongly Agree. The total score was the mean score on the items and thus is expressed on a 5-point scale. A coefficient alpha of .87 was obtained for the present study.

### Emotional Stability Measure

The emotional stability measure was taken from the same personality test used by a major consulting firm. Emotional stability was measured in terms of three subfactors: emotionality, distractibility, and energy. There were 39 items. Each item consisted of an item stem followed by a 5-step Likert scale ranging from Strongly Disagree to Strongly Agree. The total score was the mean score on the items and thus is expressed on a 5-point scale. A coefficient alpha of .90 was obtained for the present study.

### Crashes

The number of crashes was based on participant self-report for the last three years. At-fault crashes was the self-report of the number of motor vehicle crashes in which the person was at least partially at fault. Not-at-fault crashes was the self-report of the number of motor vehicle crashes in which the person was not at fault. Total crashes was the sum of at-fault crashes and not-at-fault crashes. The measure of moving violations was the self-report of the number of moving violations in the last three years.

### RESULTS

Table 1 presents the means and standard deviations, along with the correlations among the study variables. Inspection of Table 1 reveals that the only variable that was significantly correlated with any type of crashes was conscientiousness, which was negatively correlated with both not-at-fault and total crashes.

### DISCUSSION

The results of this study indicated that a personality variable, conscientiousness, was significantly correlated with total crashes and not-at-fault crashes while scores on a driving knowledge examination and on a measure of emotional stability were not significantly correlated with crashes. The significant correlations for conscientiousness were not surprising in that here conscientiousness was defined in terms of setting goals, following rules, being perfectionistic, detail-oriented, and being neat and orderly.

Although emotional stability was not significantly correlated with

TABLE 1. Descriptive Statistics and Correlations Among Study Variables

| VARIABLES | 1. | 2. | 3. | 4. | 5. | 6. | 7. |
|---|---|---|---|---|---|---|---|
| 1. Conscientiousness | -- | | | | | | |
| 2. Emotional Stability | .23 | -- | | | | | |
| 3. Driving Knowledge Test | -.06 | .13 | -- | | | | |
| 4. At-Fault Crashes | -.17 | -.12 | -.19 | -- | | | |
| 5. Not-At-Fault Crashes | -.39** | -.03 | -.03 | .12 | - | | |
| 6. Total Crashes | -.40** | -.08 | -.13 | .65*** | .83*** | - | |
| 7. Moving Violations | -.11 | -.19 | -.03 | .51 | .25* | .48*** | -- |
| Mean | 3.59 | 3.40 | 28.46 | 0.56 | 0.56 | 1.13 | 1.00 |
| SD | 0.34 | 0.47 | 4.02 | 0.71 | 0.97 | 1.27 | 1.52 |

Note: *p < .05, **p < .01, ***p < .001 (one-tailed).

the accident measures, this may have partially reflected a lack of power due to the small sample size. Perhaps with a larger sample size, the results may have reached traditional levels of statistical significance. It may also be that attention is better measured using tests of cognitive style or ability, rather than self-report personality measures (Arthur et al., 1994).

The results for the driving test were also discouraging, although again there was a low, albeit, nonsignificant correlation in the hypothesized direction between the driving knowledge test and at-fault crashes. Another problem with the driving test was that it was developed to reflect the content of the Ohio driving manual (Ohio Department of Public Safety, 1998). Much of the material in this manual dealing with laws and regulations may have had relatively little to do with crash avoidance or even safe driving. Thus, a test which reflected only those laws and regulations most germane to daily driving may have proven to be a better predictor of crash involvement.

In terms of the prevention of crashes, one could argue that in addition to testing for driving knowledge, states might consider testing drivers for their personality attributes, especially conscientiousness. One concern with this proposal is that this could be seen as involving an invasion of personal privacy. A second concern would be that it appears to be possible to fake this type of personality test, although it should be noted that faking alone may not decrease the validity of the test and could still serve as a valuable pre-screen (Barrick & Mount, 1996; Ellingson, Sackett, & Hough, 1999; Ones, Viswesvaran, &

Reiss, 1996). Certainly, drivers would be motivated to fake good. However, checks for faking could be built into the test. As an alternative to self-report inventories, video-based simulations could be used to assess a person's tendencies to make mature, rule-based driving decisions. It could also be that other indicators already used by insurance companies (e.g., grade point average) are really proxies for the measurement of conscientiousness and could be incorporated into the process of making decisions regarding the awarding of driver's licenses, especially to younger drivers.

A more realistic proposal would be to modify driver education programs so as to encourage conscientious behaviors. This would especially seem to be true when applied to younger or newer drivers. In fact, a supplemental analysis carried out on the data found that the correlations between conscientiousness and crashes were even higher for younger drivers.

The problem, and challenge for psychologists, would be to come up with training and intervention techniques for modifying what is basically a personality attribute. It would appear, however, that the behaviors associated with conscientiousness could be trained. This training could emphasize goal-setting, rule-following, and attention to detail.

## REFERENCES

Anderson, J. W. (1980). The effect of new motorcycle licensing programs and skills training on the driver records of original applicants. *Proceedings of the International Motorcycle Safety Conference*, Vol. 1.

Arthur, W., Jr., Barrett, G. V., & Alexander, R. A. (1991). Prediction of vehicular accident involvement: A meta-analysis. *Human Performance, 4*, 89-105.

Arthur, W., Jr., & Graziano, W. G. (1996). The five-factor model, conscientiousness, and driving accident involvement. *Journal of Personality, 64*, 593-618.

Arthur, W., Jr., Strong, M. H., & Williamson, J. (1994). Validation of a visual attention test as a predictor of driving accident involvement. *Journal of Occupational and Organizational Psychology, 67*, 173-182.

Barrick, M. R., & Mount, M. K. (1996). Effects of impression management and self-deception on the predictive validity of personality constructs. *Journal of Applied Psychology, 81*, 261-272.

Creech, F., & Grandy, J. (1974). *An analysis of the relationships between the renewal rules tests and the accident and violation histories*. Princeton, NJ: Educational Testing Service.

Dryer, D. R. (1976). *An evaluation of California's Driver Licensing Examination*. Sacramento: California Department of Motor Vehicles.

Elander, J., West, R., & French, D. (1993). Behavioral correlates of individual differences in road-traffic crash risk: An examination of methods and findings. *Psychological Bulletin, 113*, 279-294.

Ellingson, J. E., Sackett, P. R., & Hough, L. M. (1999). Social desirability corrections in personality measurement: Issues of applicant comparison and construct validity. *Journal of Applied Psychology, 84*, 155-166.

Goldberg, L. R. (1993). The structure of phenotypic personality traits. *American Psychologist, 48*, 26-34.

Hansen, C. P. (1989). A casual model of the relationship among accidents, biodata, personality, and cognitive factors. *Journal of Applied Psychology, 74*, 81-90.

Hill, P. S., & Jamieson, B. D. (1978). Driving offenders and the defensive driving course–An archival study. *The Journal of Psychology, 98*, 117-127.

Hogan, R. T. (1983). A socioanalytic theory of personality. In M. M. Page (ed.) *Nebraska symposium on motivation* (pp. 55-89). Lincoln, NE: University of Nebraska Press.

Hunter, J. E. (1986). Cognitive ability, cognitive demands, job knowledge, and job performance. *Journal of Vocational Behavior, 29*, 340-362.

Jonah, B. A., Dawson, N. E., & Bragg, B. W. (1981). Predicting accident involvement with the Motorcycle Operator Skill Test. *Accident Analysis and Prevention, 13*, 307-318.

Kaestner, N. (1964). *A study of licensed drivers in Oregon: Part II–Analysis of traffic involvement records*. Salem: Oregon Department of Motor Vehicles.

McCrae, R. R., & Costa, P. (1987). Validation of the five-factor model of personality across instruments and observers. *Journal of Personality and Social Psychology, 52*, 81-90.

McKnight, A. J., & Edwards, R. (1982). An experimental evaluation of driver license manuals and written tests. *Accident Analysis and Prevention, 14*, 187-192.

Ohio Department of Public Safety (1998). *Digest of Ohio motor vehicle laws*. Columbus, OH: Ohio Department of Public Safety.

Ones, D. S., Viswesvaran, C., & Reiss, A. D. (1996). Role of social desirability in personality testing for personnel selection: The red herring. *Journal of Applied Psychology, 81*, 660-679.

Parker, D., Reason, J. T., Manstead, A. S., & Stradling, S. G. (1995). Driving errors, driving violations and accident involvement. *Ergonomics, 38*, 1036-1048.

Reason, J. (1990). *Human error*. New York: Cambridge University Press.

Reason, J., Manstead, A., Stradling, S., Baxter, J., & Campbell, K. (1990). Errors and violations on the roads: A real distinction? *Ergonomics, 33*, 1315-1332.

Struckman-Johnson, D. L., Lund, A. K., Williams, A. F., & Osborne, D. W. (1989). Comparative effects of driver improvement programs on crashes and violations. *Accident Analysis and Prevention, 21*, 203-215.

Tomlinson-Keasey, C., & Little, T. D. (1990). Predicting educational attainment, occupational achievement, intellectual skill, and personal adjustment among gifted men and women. *Journal of Educational Psychology, 82*, 442-455.

# The Five-Factor Model and Safety in the Workplace: Investigating the Relationships Between Personality and Accident Involvement

Douglas F. Cellar
Zachary C. Nelson
Candice M. Yorke

DePaul University

Cara Bauer

Wayne State University

**SUMMARY.** Two hundred and two undergraduate participants (134 female, 68 male) completed both the Revised NEO Personality Inventory (NEO-PI-R) and self-report measures of prior workplace accident involvement. Significant inverse relationships were found between the factor of Agreeableness and the total reported number of work-related accidents and between the factor of Conscientiousness and the total reported number of not-at-fault work-related accidents alone, as well as the total reported number of work-related accidents. Further, regression analyses indicate that both Agreeableness and Conscientiousness factors may be useful for predicting certain types of workplace accidents. Implications and potential future directions for research are discussed. *[Article copies available for a fee from The Haworth Document Delivery Service:*

Address correspondence to: Douglas F. Cellar, Department of Psychology, DePaul University, 2219 North Kenmore Avenue, Chicago, IL 60614 or e-mail: dcellar @condor.depaul.edu.

[Haworth co-indexing entry note]: "The Five-Factor Model and Safety in the Workplace: Investigating the Relationships Between Personality and Accident Involvement." Cellar et al. Co-published simultaneously in *Journal of Prevention & Intervention in the Community* (The Haworth Press, Inc.) Vol. 22, No. 1, 2001, pp. 43-52; and: *Workplace Safety: Individual Differences in Behavior* (ed: Alice F. Stuhlmacher, and Douglas F. Cellar) The Haworth Press, Inc., 2001, pp. 43-52. Single or multiple copies of this article are available for a fee from The Haworth Document Delivery Service [1-800-342-9678, 9:00 a.m. - 5:00 p.m. (EST). E-mail address: getinfo@haworthpressinc.com].

**KEYWORDS.** Accident, Agreeableness, Conscientiousness, Five-Factor Model, NEO-PI-R, personality, safety, workplace

Because few studies have examined the relationships between personality and safety variables, the purpose of this study was to further extend this research through the use of the Five-Factor model of personality. Recently there has been a growing consensus among researchers that personality inventories based on the Five-Factor model can predict important components of training and job performance (e.g., Barrick & Mount, 1991; Tett, Jackson, & Rothstein, 1991). Tupes and Christal (1961, 1992) were the first to report a Five-Factor structure of personality, and since then, factor analytic research in both the lexical and questionnaire tradition has supported variants of the Big Five model (Cellar, Miller, Doverspike, & Klawsky, 1996; Costa & McCrae, 1985; Digman, 1990; Goldberg, 1992; Goldberg, 1993; John, 1990; Peabody, 1987; Peabody & Goldberg, 1989; Schmitt & Ryan, 1993).

According to John (1990), the five factors include Surgency or Extraversion, Agreeableness, Conscientiousness, Emotional Stability or Neuroticism, and Intellect or Openness to Experience. More recently, Costa and McCrae (1992) provided a similar description of factors. According to Costa and McCrae's Five-Factor Model (1992), Extraversion assesses the quantity and intensity of interpersonal interaction, need for stimulation, capacity for joy and activity level, Agreeableness assesses the quality of one's interpersonal orientation and Conscientiousness pertains to an individual's degree of organization, persistence, and motivation in goal-directed behavior and assesses those individuals who are fastidious and dependable. The final two factors are Neuroticism and Openness. Neuroticism assesses proneness to psychological distress, excessive urges, and maladaptive coping responses, while Openness assesses tolerance and exploration of the unfamiliar and appreciation of experiences.

While research on personality, and determination of the factors that compose it, has been extensively researched and investigated, there have been few published studies that have examined the relationships between personality and safety. Fewer still have examined these relationships from the Five-Factor perspective. In relating personality variables to driving accident involvement, Arthur, Barrett and Alexander (1991) concluded that variables such as regard for authority and locus of control exhibited moderate correlations with measures of vehicular accidents. More recently, Arthur and Graziano (1996) examined relationships between personality variables based on the Five-Factor Model and driving accident behavior. They found that individuals who rated themselves higher in Conscientiousness were involved in fewer driving accidents.

In terms of investigating other types of work-related accidents, studies have found personality variables to be predictive of the tendency to engage in such behavior. Hansen (1989), for instance, found scales based on the Minnesota Multiphasic Personality Inventory (MMPI) were predictive of accidents for workers in the chemical industry, and labeled the scales he created Social Maladjustment and Distractibility. In addition, other studies have shown personality variables to be related to workplace accidents (Borofsky & Smith, 1993; Brown & Berdies, 1960; Harrell, 1995; Janicak, 1996; Jones & Wuebker, 1988) and recent reviews of the personality and safety literature have been optimistic regarding the utility of using such measures to screen applicants (Borofsky & Smith, 1993; Furnham, 1992; Hansen, 1988; Kamp & Krause, 1997).

There are a number of traits and other variables that have been related to personality in safety literature. For example, Borofsky and Smith (1993) employed the Employee Reliability Scale (ERI) which consisted of six scales (freedom from disruptive alcohol and substance use; emotional maturity, conscientiousness, trustworthiness, long-term job commitment and safe job performance) to help predict rates of accidents, turnover and absenteeism. Harrell (1995) looked at the relationship between experience, risk-taking, belief that accidents were inevitable and accident involvement and recommended the use of psychological variables for studying occupational accidents and attitudes toward safety. Locus of control has also been a variable of interest and it has been suggested that when examined in conjunction with job hazard variables, it may be a good predictor of workplace accidents (Janicak, 1996).

As a result, it is suggested that through the further exploration of the relationships between personality variables and safety from a five-factor perspective, a more coherent view of the area will emerge. Overall, it seems that based on past research the facets of Conscientiousness, Neuroticism, Extraversion and Agreeableness may be related to accident behavior in the workplace. An additional advantage of using the Five-Factor model as a theoretical guide for this type of research is that the behavioral patterns associated with the factors are well known in comparison to the large number of specific factors that have been identified in the literature.

The measures of accident involvement used in this study were self-report in nature, and as suggested by current research that has investigated driving accident involvement (Arthur et al., 1999), such self-report data may be just as accurate, if not more accurate, than archival data. Specifically, driving accident research has indicated that accidents may be under-reported to authorities, and archival records may be incomplete (Burns & Wilde, 1995; McGuire, 1973; Smith, 1976). As a result of these findings, it might be possible to conclude that work-related accidents may be similarly under-reported to the organization or other authorities. Because this study was interested in measuring all types of accidents, regardless of severity, the use of self-report data was deemed most appropriate.

The present study attempted to extend the existing research on personality and safety behavior in the workplace. The relationship between personality, as measured by the NEO-PI-R (Costa & McCrae, 1992), and workplace accident involvement was examined. The value of this research lies in the fact that once such relationships are established, personality inventories may then be used to predict individuals who are more likely to behave safely. In addition, broad behavioral patterns that are related to the personality characteristics can be identified. Such information would have important implications for selection and for enhancing the effectiveness of behaviorally based safety training programs.

## *METHOD*

### *Participants*

Two hundred and two university undergraduates (134 female, 68 male) enrolled in lower division psychology courses at a private Midwestern university in the United States participated in this study for partial fulfillment of course requirements. The average age of the participants was indicative of an undergraduate sample ($M$ = 20.93, $SD$ = 4.96) and the ethnic backgrounds of the participants were representative of the racial diversity of the institution, including the following: 60.4% Caucasian, 13.4% Hispanic, 12.4% African Americans, 9.4% Asian Americans, 1.5% Native American and 3% other ethnic identities. One hundred and forty of the participants (69.3%) held a job at the time of the study, but all participants indicated they had held a job at some point and the length of time they had been working in general ranged from less than one year to twenty-five years ($M$ = 4.9, $SD$ = 4.1).

## *Measures*

Each participant completed the *Revised NEO Personality Inventory* (NEO-PI-R: Costa & McCrae, 1992), as well as a work safety behavior questionnaire designed to assess personal safety behavior in the workplace. This measure was adapted from a driving accident measure used by Arthur and Graziano (1996) to apply to accident involvement in the workplace. The NEO-PI-R consisted of 240 statements for which participants were asked to indicate agreement through the use of a 5-point Likert-type scale ranging from "strongly disagree" to "strongly agree." Coefficient alpha for each of the five factors as reported by Costa and McCrae (1992) indicate good levels of reliability for each of the factors (Neuroticism = .92, Extraversion = .89, Openness = .87, Agreeableness = .86, Conscientiousness = .90). As expected, factor reliabilities in this study were consistent (Neuroticism = .90, Extraversion = .87, Openness = .89, Agreeableness = .87, Conscientiousness = .90).

For the workplace accident measure, participants were asked to indicate separately both the number of at-fault and not-at-fault work-related accidents they had been involved in in each of the past ten years (1988-1998). "At-fault" accidents were defined as any accident the participant was involved in in which he/she personally was at fault. Conversely, "not-at fault" accidents were defined as those the participant was involved in, but were not caused by their own negligence. For the purpose of this study, participants were asked to report all accidents that had caused injury to the self. Participants were instructed that to qualify as an "accident," the incident did not necessarily have to have caused significant personal injury. Participants were told that such accidents might include cutting oneself on a piece of machinery, a slip on a wet floor, or spraining an ankle or wrist. Prior to the administration of these two measures, participants provided demographic information including age, gender, year in school, grade point average, ethnicity and whether or not they held a job at the time of the study.

## Procedure

Following the completion of a signed and dated consent form, participants were presented with the NEO-PI-R, followed by the self-report measure of workplace accident involvement. Participants were run in small groups of up to five individuals per group. On average, measures took between forty-five minutes to one hour for participants to complete. At the end of the session, participants were debriefed, informed of the nature of the study, given relevant references, and were asked to remain following the experiment if any questions remained.

## RESULTS

Analyses examined the correlations between each of the five personality factors, work "at-fault" accidents and work "not-at-fault" accidents, and the total number of accidents (sum of "at-fault" and "not-at-fault"). Additional regression analyses were run in an effort to test the extent to which the personality factors could predict accident involvement. As presented in Table 1, the total number of "at-fault" workplace accidents reported by participants over the ten-year period ranged from 0-24 accidents ($M = 0.63$, $SD = 2.75$). The total number of "not-at-fault" workplace accidents reported ranged from 0-52 accidents over the ten-year period ($M = 0.59$, $SD = 3.78$). Table 1 shows that, of the five factors, a significant inverse correlation was found between Conscientiousness and both the sum of the total "not-at-fault" accidents reported ($r = -.14$, $p < .05$) and total "at-fault" and "not-at-fault" accidents combined ($r = -.16$, $p < .05$). In addition, a significant inverse correlation was found between Agreeableness and the sum of both total "at-fault" and "not-at-fault" accidents ($r = -.13$, $p < .05$). No significant relationships were found between the factors of Openness, Extraversion and Neuroticism and accident involvement.

In addition to these correlational results, regression analyses were conducted in an effort to investigate the degree to which the five personality factors could be used to predict accident involvement. Specifically, stepwise linear regression analyses indicated that Conscientiousness alone was a good predictor of both the number of not-at-fault workplace accidents $F$ (1, 201) = 3.94, $p < .05$ ($R^2 = .019$) and the sum of both at-fault and not-at-fault workplace accidents $F$ (1, 201) = 5.02, $p < .05$ ($R^2 = .024$). In addition, when Agreeableness was entered into the model predicting total work accidents, a $\Delta R^2$ of .009 was found, and the model remained a statistically significant predictor of total workplace accidents $F$ (2, 201) = 3.39, $p < .05$ ($R^2 = .033$). Based on these results, it seems that Agreeableness does not explain much incremental variance beyond that found with Conscientiousness alone. Based on the strong correlation between Conscientiousness and Agreeableness, it is not surprising that there seems to be a great deal of common variance between the two personality factors, given their relationship with each other.

## DISCUSSION

Taken as a whole these results indicated the moderate relationships between certain personality factors and safe behavior in the workplace. This study shows that Conscientiousness and Agreeableness as measured by the NEO-PI-R were significantly negatively correlated

TABLE 1. Means, Standard Deviations and Correlation Matrix

| | M | SD | (1) | (2) | (3) | (4) | (5) | (6) | (7) | (8) |
|---|---|---|---|---|---|---|---|---|---|---|
| (1)Agreeableness | 111.37 | 18.31 | — — | | | | | | | |
| (2)Conscientiousness | 111.87 | 19.81 | .25** | — — | | | | | | |
| (3)Extraversion | 122.01 | 18.37 | .09 | .25** | — — | | | | | |
| (4)Neuroticism | 99.52 | 21.29 | −.28** | −.45** | −.29** | — — | | | | |
| (5)Openness | 126.77 | 19.71 | .23** | −.01 | −.38** | .09 | — — | | | |
| (6)Total Work At-Fault Accidents | .63 | 2.75 | −.07 | −.08 | −.06 | .07 | −.11 | — — | | |
| (7)Total Work Not-At-Fault Accidents | .59 | 3.78 | −.11 | −.14* | .04 | .03 | .08 | .02 | — — | |
| (8)Combined Total At-Fault and Not-At-Fault | 1.23 | 4.72 | −.13* | −.16* | −.01 | .06 | −.00 | .60** | .81** | — — |

$N$ = 202. * $p < .05$, one-tailed.** $p < .01$, one-tailed.

with the total number of "at-fault" and "not-at-fault" accidents experienced in the workplace, while Conscientiousness was significantly negatively correlated with "not-at-fault" accidents alone. Regression results suggest that these two personality factors may be useful for helping to predict accident involvement in the workplace.

One potential limitation of this study may be that it was conducted with an undergraduate sample with a mean age of around twenty years and hence, with potentially limited work experience. Previous studies (Janicak, 1996) have required participants to have held a full-time position for the number of years in which workplace accidents were analyzed in an effort to ensure more consistency and accuracy especially when the measure of accidents is archival (e.g., number of worker's compensation claims filed). However, in the present study, since all workplace accidents, major and minor, and not just those formally reported, were of interest, our sample still clearly illustrates the significant relationship between workplace accident involvement and personality. Thus, while the present results may be restricted somewhat due to the limited work experience of the sample, the significant findings with respect to Conscientiousness, and to a lesser degree, Agreeableness, point to the fact that the relationships found might be especially pronounced in an older adult population. Given the support for self-report data in literature (Arthur et al., 1999), it is clear that future studies investigating similar relationships between personality and safety may find self-report data most appropriate, either by itself, or in conjunction with archival safety records to achieve a most complete measure of workplace accident involvement.

It is clear that the results from this study point to the strong relationship between personality and work-related safety behaviors. Through the extension of safety research to include the Five-Factor Model of personality, it is evident that established personality inventories might be useful for predicting work-related accident behavior by identifying broad behavioral patterns related to safety. Because of this, the implications for using such measures to help understand and pinpoint these patterns are that training programs can be directed toward targeting behavioral change as opposed to attempting to change the traits of individuals, which is likely to be much more difficult. As a result, personality inventories may be very useful for helping to select individuals who are most likely to behave safely in the workplace through the traits and behaviors associated with these traits that they are likely to exhibit. In turn, using personality measures to aid training development may serve to minimize the number of workplace accidents, something that is of significant benefit to organizations and employees alike.

## REFERENCES

Arthur, W., Jr., Barrett, G.V., & Alexander, R.A. (1991). Prediction of vehicular accident involvement: A meta-analysis. *Human Performance, 4*, 89-105.

Arthur, W., Jr., & Graziano, W.G. (1996). The five-factor model, conscientiousness, and driving accident involvement. *Journal of Personality, 64*, 593-618.

Arthur, W., Jr., Tubre, T., Sheehan, M. K., Sanchez-Ku, M., Day, E. A., Paul, D., Paulus, L., & Archuleta, K. (1999). *Convergence of Self-Report and Archival Data in the Prediction of Motor Vehicle Crash Involvement and Moving Violations.* Manuscript submitted for publication.

Barrick, M.R., & Mount, M.K. (1991). The big five personality dimensions and job performance: A meta-analysis. *Personnel Psychology, 44*, 1-26.

Borofsky, G.L., & Smith, M. (1993). Reductions in turnover, accidents, and absenteeism: The contribution of a pre-employment screening inventory. *Journal of Clinical Psychology, 49*, 109-116.

Brown, P.L., & Berdies, R.F. (1960). Driver behavior and scores on the MMPI. *Journal of Applied Psychology, 44*, 18-21.

Burns, P. C., & Wilde, G. J. S. (1995). Risk taking in male taxi drivers: Relationships among personality, observational data and driver records. *Personality and Individual Differences, 18*, 267-278.

Cellar, D.F., Miller, M.L., Doverspike, D.D., & Klawsky, J.D. (1996). Comparison of factor structures and criterion-related validity coefficients for two measures of personality based on the factor model. *Journal of Applied Psychology, 81*, 694-704.

Costa, P.T., Jr., & McCrae, R.R. (1985). *The NEO Personality Inventory Manual.* Odessa, FL: Psychological Assessment Resources.

Costa, P.T., Jr., & McCrae, R.R. (1992). *The NEO Personality Inventory Manual.* Odessa, FL: Psychological Assessment Resources.

Digman, J.M. (1990). Personality structure: Emergence of the five-factor model. *Annual Review of Psychology, 41*, 417-440.

Furnham, A. (1992). *Personality at work: The role of individual differences in the workplace.* London: Routledge.

Goldberg, L.R. (1992). The development of markers for the Big-Five factor structure. *Psychological Assessment, 4*, 26-42.

Goldberg, L.R. (1993). The structure of phenotypic personality traits. *American Psychologist, 48*, 26-34.

Hansen, C.P. (1988). Personality characteristics of the accident involved employee. *Journal of Business and Psychology, 2*, 346-365.

Hansen, C.P. (1989). A causal model of the relationship among accidents, biodata, personality, and cognitive factors. *Journal of Applied Psychology, 74*, 81-90.

Harrell, W.A. (1995). Factors influencing involvement in farm accidents. *Perceptual and Motor Skills, 81*, 592-594.

Janicak, C.A. (1996). Predicting accidents at work with measures of locus of control and job hazards. *Psychological Reports, 78*, 115-121.

John, O.P. (1990). The "Big Five" factor taxonomy: Dimensions of personality in the natural language and in questionnaires. In L.A. Pervin (Ed.) *Handbook of personality theory and research* (pp. 66-100). New York: Guilford Press.

Jones, J.W., & Wuebker, L.J. (1988). Accident prevention through personnel selection. *Journal of Business and Psychology, 3*, 187-198.

Kamp, J., & Krause, T.R. (1997, April). Selecting safe employees: A behavioral science perspective. *Professional Safety.*

McGuire, F. L. (1973). The nature of bias in official accident and violation records. *Journal of Applied Psychology, 57*, 300-305.

Peabody, D. (1987). Selecting representative trait adjectives. *Journal of Personality and Social Psychology, 52*, 59-71.

Peabody, D., & Goldberg, L.R. (1989). Some determinants of factor structures from personality-trait descriptors. *Journal of Personality and Social Psychology, 57*, 352-567.

Schmitt, M. J., & Ryan, A. M. (1993). The Big Five in personnel selection: Factor structure in applicant and nonapplicant populations. *Journal of Applied Psychology, 78*, 966-974.

Smith, D. I. (1976). Official driver records and self-reports as sources of accident and conviction data for research purposes. *Accident Prevention and Analysis, 8*, 207-211.

Tett, R.P., Jackson, D.N., & Rothstein, M. (1991). Personality measures as predictors of job performance: A meta-analytic review. *Personnel Psychology, 44*, 703-742.

Tupes, E.C., & Christal, R.E. (1961). *Recurrent personality factors based on trait ratings* (USAF ASD Tech. Rep. No. 61-97). Lackland Air Force Base, TX: U.S. Air Force.

Tupes, E.C., & Christal, R.E. (1992). Recurrent personality factors based on trait ratings. *Journal of Personality, 60*, 225-251.

# Creating a Safer Working Environment Through Psychological Assessment: A Review of a Measure of Safety Consciousness

Bradford H. Forcier
Amy E. Walters
Eric E. Brasher
John W. Jones

NCS-Pearson

**SUMMARY.** This article explores how organizations can prevent workplace accidents through the psychological assessment of employees. We present a model of employee safety consciousness consisting of personality and attitudinal variables associated with a higher risk of accident involvement. A safety conscious employee is described as one who: has an internal locus of control in matters related to workplace safety, has a high tolerance for work-related stress, and avoids engaging in high-risk, sensation-seeking activities. Relevant research is reviewed and applications of the safety consciousness construct to hiring, promotion and training are discussed. *[Article copies available for a fee from The Haworth Document Delivery Service: 1-800-342-9678. E-mail address: <getinfo@haworthpressinc.com> Website: <http://www.HaworthPress.com> © 2001 by The Haworth Press, Inc. All rights reserved.]*

Address correspondence to: Bradford H. Forcier, NCS, 9701 W. Higgins Road, Rosemont, IL 60018.

[Haworth co-indexing entry note]: "Creating a Safer Working Environment Through Psychological Assessment: A Review of a Measure of Safety Consciousness." Forcier et al. Co-published simultaneously in *Journal of Prevention & Intervention in the Community* (The Haworth Press, Inc.) Vol. 22, No. 1, 2001, pp. 53-65; and: *Workplace Safety: Individual Differences in Behavior* (ed: Alice F. Stuhlmacher, and Douglas F. Cellar) The Haworth Press, Inc., 2001, pp. 53-65. Single or multiple copies of this article are available for a fee from The Haworth Document Delivery Service [1-800-342-9678, 9:00 a.m. - 5:00 p.m. (EST). E-mail address: getinfo@haworthpressinc.com].

**KEYWORDS.** Accident potential, accident reduction, employee safety inventory, locus of control, personnel assessment, risk avoidance, safety, safety consciousness, sensation-seeking, stress tolerance

Taken at once, the array of dangers found in the workplace can be overwhelming. In any given job workers may face environmental hazards posed by heavy machinery, wet surfaces, sharp edges or hazardous materials. Situational variables like dangerous heights, extreme temperatures, heavy lifting or driving also present safety risks. Almost every job has some risk exposure, and although annual figures of company and personal losses resulting from workplace accidents are steadily decreasing (Gaboury, 1998), the prevention of such accidents remains an appropriately high priority for many companies.

Organizations seeking to reduce the frequency and severity of workplace accidents often take more than one approach to the problem. A fundamental component of many programs is incorporating safety features into the design of equipment and in the layout of organizational facilities. Training employees who work with dangerous equipment or perform hazardous tasks to follow established safety protocols accomplishes another mainstay of safety initiatives. To ensure the effectiveness of safety training, programs should incorporate at least short-term monitoring of employee behaviors combined with feedback reinforcing established protocol and encouraging continued safe work behaviors. However, recent trends in hierarchical structure and associated organizational dynamics have made it increasingly more difficult for organizations to provide adequate monitoring and feedback. Flatter organizational structures, wider spans of control, self-managed work groups, and flexible work schedules result in fewer opportunities for management to observe and correct violations of safety codes. Thus, organizations are being forced to rely upon employees' capacity for self-regulation to manage behavior. This increased reliance upon self-regulation underscores the need for truly comprehensive workplace safety strategies that appreciate and address the human factors that precipitate accidents.

This article describes a psychological measure of employee safety consciousness that can be used by organizations to incorporate assessment of safety-related human factors into a comprehensive risk reduction strategy. The paper includes a brief exploration of the general concept of safety consciousness followed by a definitive explanation of the safety consciousness construct. Following a review of the three key components of the construct, a measure of safety consciousness is described along with research demonstrating its effectiveness in predicting workplace accidents and unsafe behavior. Finally, applications of the safety consciousness measures to employee selection, promotion, and training will be discussed.

## Safety Consciousness

In the broadest sense, safety consciousness refers to the values, attitudes and beliefs that underlie the awareness of safety hazards and the ability to handle potentially dangerous situations effectively. A fundamental assumption in the conceptualization of safety consciousness is that certain individuals have a greater probability of being involved in a workplace accident than others, and that these individuals differ in not just safe work behaviors, but in the values, attitudes and beliefs that manifest those behaviors.

The view that some individuals are more likely to be involved in accidents than others is not new to the field. Contemplation of the "accident-prone" personality can be found in literature published as early as 1918 (Vernon). Today it is widely acknowledged that the majority of accidents are precipitated by some form of human error (Kamp, 1994). In a review of literature on individual differences in accident potential, Hansen (1991) identified several personality characteristics that have been found to be associated with a higher risk of being involved in an accident. Specifically, the review suggests that individuals with high accident potential tend to be extroverted, aggressive, socially maladjusted, neurotic, impulsive, and tend to have an external locus of control when it comes to preventing accidents in the workplace.

The finding that workplace accidents may be attributable, in part, to personality differences has important implications for organizations interested in promoting a safe work environment. To the extent that these differences can be measured, organizations can reduce the risk of workplace accidents by making more informed decisions in employee hiring, placement and training needs assessment. To do this, however, organizations need a clear understanding of the essential employee characteristics that contribute to safe work practices. While research has demonstrated that a broad variety of traits empirically predict accident involvement, it is not practical to assess employees on all of these characteristics. What is needed is a concise theoretical framework outlining the core characteristics of the safety-oriented worker.

In this paper, we present an applied model of safety consciousness. Rather than a comprehensive model of the accident-prone personality type, our conceptualization of safety consciousness will focus on three key attitudinal measures that have broad implications and relevance to preventing industrial accidents: safety locus of control, risk avoidance and stress tolerance. Although they are intercorrelated, we assert that each measure makes a distinct contribution to the overall safety consciousness of the individual (Figure 1). Further discussion of the development and implications of each measure is presented below.

*Safety locus of control.* Few theories in the modern study of psychology have been as broadly applied as Rotter's theory of locus of control (1966). The locus of control concept refers to the degree to which individuals believe self-determination operates in their lives. Individuals with an external locus of control are likely to view the things that happen in their lives as being due to chance, luck, or destiny. Those with an internal locus of control are more likely to perceive personal attributes and effort as the determining factors in most life events.

Safety locus of control refers specifically to an individual's locus of control in matters related to avoiding workplace accidents (Jones & Wuebker, 1985). That is, an individual with an external safety locus of control does not feel personally responsible for accidents and does not believe that he or she has the power to control them. It follows that such an individual would expend little energy in taking safety precautions, thereby posing a greater safety risk to themselves and their co-workers. Conversely, an individual with an internal safety locus of control will tend to feel personally responsible for their safety and take preventative steps to avoid accidents and injuries. The safety locus of control scale has a higher degree of face validity than could be achieved by using Rotter's original scale because it is based on individual perceptions of life experiences that are specific to safe work behaviors. As such, the safety locus of control scale is more appropriate for use in occupational settings.

*Risk avoidance.* The concept of risk avoidance stems from Zuckerman's (1971, 1979) theory of sensation-seeking. According to Zuckerman, sensation-seeking refers to an individual's need for excitement, variety and intense stimulation, coupled with the willingness to take

FIGURE 1. Key Attitudinal Measures of Safety Consciousness

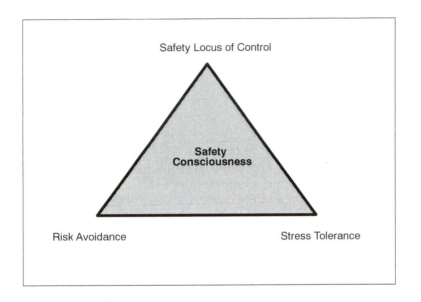

risks to have such experiences. High sensation-seekers are drawn to adventurous and even dangerous activities, both external and internal in nature. They also exhibit a lack of inhibition and are highly susceptible to boredom. Risk avoidance, on the other hand, is characterized by a lack of sensation-seeking tendencies. High risk avoidance individuals are more comfortable in highly structured environments and situations with relatively low stimulation levels. Because of their preference for structure, high risk avoidance individuals are also more likely to follow established safety protocols and are less susceptible to boredom.

*Stress tolerance.* The construct of stress tolerance refers to an individual's ability to contend with stress of a situational and temporary nature. Many occupations are characterized by "rush" periods such as the lunch hour for restaurant staff, or an unusually aggressive production goal in a manufacturing environment. During these rush periods the level of stress is increased as the individual worker is forced to work faster than usual while giving adequate attention to an increased number of competing demands. All employees experience stress, but some are more likely to react in ways that lead to mistakes and errors.

According to Jones, DuBois, and Wuebker (1986), these negative stress reactions may be mental (e.g., inattentiveness, confusion, poor judgment, indecision, impaired perceptions), emotional (e.g., frustration, anger, impulsiveness, carelessness), and physical (e.g., fatigue, tension).

In times of peak job demands, individuals low in stress tolerance are more likely to become flustered or frantic and experience a reduction in both the quality and breadth of their focus and attention. Over time, they may even begin to exhibit recurring physical reactions (Jones, DuBois, & Wuebker, 1986). Conversely, individuals who have high stress tolerance are more likely to recover quickly from peak job demand periods, and are more able to remain cool, focused and attentive during times of increased pressure and stress.

*The safety conscious employee: A summary.* Safety locus of control, risk avoidance, and stress tolerance comprise a three-faceted conceptualization of the safety consciousness construct. In summary, the safety conscious individual is likely to take more responsibility for his or her own safety, less likely to engage in risky behaviors, and less susceptible to risks associated with periods of peak job demands. Possessing an internal safety locus of control, the individual perceives that his or her actions will be effective in preventing workplace accidents. A preference for structure and predictability makes the safety conscious individual less likely to engage in unnecessarily risky, dangerous or thrill-seeking behaviors that contribute to workplace accidents. Finally, the safety conscious individual is more resilient when faced with situational determinants of safety hazards as he or she has the ability to remain calm and focused during a temporary escalation of job demands.

## Validity of a Safety Consciousness Measure

Having presented the framework of the safety consciousness construct, we will now review research evidence suggesting that safety locus of control, risk avoidance and stress tolerance are effective in distinguishing between employees with high and low risk of accident involvement. The research reviewed here is predominantly from validation studies of the Employee Safety Inventory (ESI®) assessment, developed and supported by NCS. The ESI assessment is a psychological instrument that utilizes the safety locus of control, risk avoidance and stress tolerance scales to calculate an overall Safety Index. Scale reliabilities and intercorrelations of the ESI are given in Table 1. The ESI assessment also includes a scale called Driver Attitudes that is not used in the calculation of the composite score. This scale is primarily derived from the concept of safety locus of control applied to driving situations. It provides supplemental information regarding an individual's propensity to consistently engage in safe driving practices. Two other scales, Validity/Distortion and Validity/Accuracy, are included to verify the credibility of the scores. A low Validity/Distortion score indicates that an individual may have tried to answer questions in a manner he or she perceived to be socially desirable. A low Validity/ Accuracy score indicates that a respondent did not understand the questions adequately, or was careless in completing the assessment.

*Safety Control.* As discussed earlier, the Safety Control scale of the ESI assessment measures whether an individual has an internal or external locus of control in matters related to workplace safety. A higher score on this scale indicates a more internal orientation. The safety control scale has been shown to be related to employees' accident histories in a wide assortment of jobs and industrial environments. Rafilson and Rospenda (1989) classified 161 employees of a major manufacturing company as having good or poor safety records on the basis of their personnel files. Employees with "good" safety records had no work-related injuries in the past five years. A "poor" safety record was characterized by two or more work-related injuries in the past three years. It was found that employees with good safety records had significantly higher Safety Control scores. Results similar to these have also been obtained in the hotel, grocery, and transportation industries (Wuebker, Jones, & Dubois, 1986; Jones & Slora, 1988; Boye, Joy, Slora & Jones, 1990). Among 283 hospital employees, Jones and Wuebker (1985) found that individuals with high Safety Control reported having less work-related injuries and lower medical costs resulting from injury. Finally, Jones and Foreman (1984) found that bus driver applicants with an external safety locus of control had more offenses for unsafe driving practices on their State Motor Vehicle Reports.

In a study of the predictive potential of Safety Control, Jones and Slora (1988) administered the assessment to 380 grocery store applicants that were subsequently hired using the organization's normal procedures. After three months on the job, employee safety records were examined. It was found that employees with no work-related

TABLE 1. Scale Reliabilities* and Intercorrelations of the ESI

| Scale | 1. | 2. | 3. |
|-------|-----|-----|-----|
| 1. Safety Control | .85 | .65 | .67 |
| 2. Risk Avoidance | – | .80 | .61 |
| 3. Stress Tolerance | – | – | .81 |

*reliability coefficients appear in the diagonal

accidents had significantly higher Safety Control scores than employees who had been involved in a workplace accident during the same time period.

*Risk Avoidance.* The Risk Avoidance scale of the ESI® assessment measures an individual's tendency to engage in high-risk, thrill-seeking or dangerous activities. Low scores on the assessment are indicative of a more sensation-seeking orientation. Risk Avoidance scores appear to be related to a number of thrill-seeking and counterproductive behaviors that have implications for workplace safety. For example, several studies have investigated the relationship between Risk Avoidance and unsafe driving behavior. In a study by Boye, Slora, and Molcan (1989), pizza delivery drivers completed a questionnaire in which they were asked to indicate the frequency of their unsafe driving behaviors (e.g., speeding, drinking and driving, accidents). On the basis of these self-ratings, drivers were classified into "safe" and "unsafe" driving groups. The groups were found to differ in their Risk Avoidance scores, with "safe" drivers having significantly higher scores than "unsafe" drivers. Risk Avoidance scores were also found to be significantly related to admissions of drinking and driving by drivers of a large dairy processing company (Slora, Boye, & Jones, 1989).

Jones, Britton, and Slora (1988) found significant relationships between Risk Avoidance scores and the self-reported frequency of drug and alcohol use among college students. Individuals scoring low in Risk Avoidance indicated a higher frequency of drug and alcohol use in a typical month and a higher frequency of on the job drug and alcohol use. Risk Avoidance has also been found to have a significant, negative correlation with self-reported absences and illegal activity, and supervisory ratings of tardiness (Behrens, Slora, & Jones, 1988). Furthermore, Risk Avoidance scores correlate with two scales of the

MMPI that have been found to be predictive of accident potential: General Social Maladjustment and Distractibility (Hansen, 1991; Slora, Boye, & Jones, 1991).

*Stress Tolerance.* The Stress Tolerance scale of the ESI® assessment measures an individual's ability to withstand stress, with high scores indicating a greater tolerance for stressful situations. Several studies have shown this scale to be a useful tool in identifying potential for accident involvement. Slora and Molcan (1990) administered the ESI to 257 warehouse employees of a large retailing company. One week later, supervisors rated the employees' performance on a standardized evaluation checklist. It was found that employee Stress Tolerance scores were positively correlated with supervisors' ratings of safety knowledge, safe work behaviors, and emotional control. Other studies have shown significant relationships between Stress Tolerance and safe driving behaviors of delivery drivers (Boye, Slora, & Molcan, 1989).

Like Risk Avoidance, Stress Tolerance appears to be related to a number of work behaviors that have implications for workplace safety. Individuals with high tolerance for stress are rated by their supervisors as being more dependable, more accepting of responsibility, and more organized (Halverson, Orban, & Behrens, 1989). Other studies have shown relationships between Stress Tolerance scores and supervisory ratings of the employee's amount of job interest and motivation (Halverson & Behrens, 1989). In addition, individuals scoring high in Stress Tolerance tend to have lower scores on the MMPI's General Social Maladjustment and Distractibility scales (Slora, Boye, & Jones, 1991).

## Applications for a Measure of Safety Consciousness

Thus far, we have argued that individual differences in personality, attitudes and beliefs contribute to an employee's ability to effectively handle potential safety hazards. Research and theory relating to three of these individual difference variables were reviewed in order to substantiate a model of employee safety consciousness. Having defined the model, we will now discuss how the safety consciousness construct can be applied to reducing risk in the workplace. In particular, we will address the role of safety consciousness as an integrated component of a selection process, as supplemental information in making promotion decisions, and in training needs assessment.

*Selection.* For safety sensitive positions, the selection process is the first line of defense an organization has against hiring unsafe workers. Incorporating safety consciousness into the hiring process is particularly beneficial since hiring decisions are often based on relatively limited amounts of information from a modest number of sources. Standardized applications can qualify pertinent experience, and structured interviews present an opportunity to interact with prospective employees and to gauge response content to specific job relevant topics. When implemented between the application and interview process, a psychological assessment of safety consciousness can provide an objective hurdle, or help guide a follow-up interview. Whether high-risk candidates are screened out or receive further consideration only for low risk positions, the inclusion of safety consciousness in the selection process ultimately expands the breadth of information available for making hiring and placement decisions.

The effectiveness of safety consciousness as a component of a selection process can be best realized through a consistent and sustained program. A sustained program increases the likelihood that the employee population will reach a point of "saturation" when the proportion of workers screened in and/or placed using the assessment reaches a point of critical mass and begins to impact organizational culture. In addition, the emphasis placed on safety in an organization's culture can be further reinforced through HR initiatives related to promotion and training.

*Promotion.* Although any psychological assessments should be appropriately weighted against job performance history and other matters of record, safety consciousness does offer a perspective and insight not captured by traditional performance measures. For example, safety consciousness could help distinguish the most desirable candidate from two or more individuals who are similarly qualified candidates in terms of traditional performance indicators. Evaluation of safety consciousness could also be helpful when the position being filled is highly safety sensitive, or is a supervisory role overseeing subordinates in safety sensitive positions. As a purely objective measurement, safety consciousness is not effected by supervisor bias, and can provide avenues of inquiry during subsequent interviews and evaluations.

*Training and development.* Safety consciousness can also be used to identify specific individual training and development needs, and can serve as a guide to the development of departmental or company level training programs. For instance, training modules can be developed to address specific elements of safety consciousness. A training module addressing low safety control might incorporate behavioral modeling and job simulation exercises to increase employees' perception of control in their environment. A training module addressing low stress tolerance might emphasize how to quickly recognize situations and emotional responses that can distract workers from paying adequate attention to safety. For many individuals, simply learning about the different attitudes and perspectives that are associated with safety consciousness can result in a higher awareness of their role in creating a safe work environment.

A process called organizational risk assessment can yield similar guidance at the group, department or company level. The organizational risk assessment procedure involves aggregating individual safety-related measures, the result of which reflects the cultural atmosphere shared by the individuals in the studied group. These results are used in a similar fashion as those obtained for individuals; the only difference is that the target for training is the studied group as opposed to any single worker.

## *CONCLUSION*

In this paper we presented a framework of the safety consciousness construct. Briefly, safety conscious workers: (1) believe they can prevent accidents from happening, (2) avoid engaging in unnecessarily risky behaviors and (3) are not in overly challenged stressful situations.

Considering the staggering monetary, physical and emotional costs of workplace accidents, it seems compelling that businesses should take initiatives to investigate and evaluate every possible option in the prevention of employee accidents. We have explored how organizations can facilitate and foster a safe work environment by assessing and developing safety consciousness in the workforce. While we have emphasized an approach to workplace safety based on individual differences, it is important to recognize that this is only one approach to a complex, multi-faceted issue. However, we assert that psychological assessment in general, and that the safety consciousness construct in particular, can be an effective component of a comprehensive program designed to promote occupational safety.

## REFERENCES

Behrens, G. M., Slora, K. B., & Jones, J. W. (1988). *Construct validity of a standard-ized measure of risk avoidance.* ESI Research Abstract No. 4. Rosemont, IL: National Computer Systems.

Boye, M. W., Joy, D. S., Slora, K. B., & Jones, J. W. (1990). *The relation of the Employee Safety Inventory to driving accidents and related costs at a national trucking company.* ESI Technical Report No. 13. Rosemont, IL: National Computer Systems.

Boye, M. W., Slora, K. B. & Molcan, J. R. (1989). *The relation of the Employee Safety Inventory to safe driving behaviors among pizza delivery employees.* ESI Research Abstract No. 12. Rosemont, IL: National Computer Systems.

Gaboury, J. (1998). Workplace injury, illness decrease. *IIE Solutions*, 30 (10), 8.

Halverson, R. R., & Behrens, G. M. (1989). *Prediction of successful customer service representatives using the Telemarketing Applicant Inventory.* TMAI Technical Report No. 2. Rosemont, IL: National Computer Systems.

Halverson, R. R., Orban, J. A. & Behrens, G. M. (1989). *Prediction of current telemarketer performance using the Telemarketing Applicant Inventory.* TMAI Technical Report No. 1. Rosemont, IL: National Computer Systems.

Hansen, C. P. (1991). Personality characteristics of the accident-involved employee. In J. Jones, B. Steffy, & D. Bray (Eds.), *Applying psychology in business* (pp. 801-812). New York: Lexington Books.

Jones, J. W., Britton, C. F., & Slora, K. B. (1988). *The relation of the Employee Safety Inventory to drug and alcohol use.* ESI Research Abstract No. 2. Rosemont, IL: National Computer Systems.

Jones, J. W., DuBois, D., & Wuebker, L. J. (1986). Promoting safety by reducing human error. *Personnel*, 63, 41-44.

Jones, J. W., & Foreman, R. J. (1984). *Relationship of PSI Safety Scale scores to motor vehicle reports.* PSI Technical Report No. 58. Rosemont, IL: National Computer Systems.

Jones, J. W., & Slora, K. B. (1988). *Predictive validation study of the Safety Control Scale.* ESI Research Abstract No. 1. Rosemont, IL: National Computer Systems.

Jones, J. W., & Wuebker, L. J. (1985). Development and validation of the Safety Locus of Control Scale. *Perceptual and Motor Skills, 61*, 151-161.

Kamp, J. (1994, May). Worker psychology: Safety management's next frontier. *Professional Safety,* 32-36.

Rafilson, F. M. & Rospenda, K. M. (1989). *Concurrent validation study of the Safety scale.* PSI Technical Report No. 84. Rosemont, IL: National Computer Systems.

Rotter, J. B. (1966). Generalized expectancies for internal versus external locus of control. *Psychological Monographs*, 80, 1 (Whole no. 609).

Slora, K. B., Boye, M. W., & Jones, J. W. (1988). *Construct validation study of the Employee Safety Inventory.* ESI Research Abstract No. 3. Rosemont, IL: National Computer Systems.

Slora, K. B., Boye, M. W., & Jones, J. W. (1989). *The relation of the Employee Safety Inventory to safe driving behaviors among delivery drivers.* ESI Research Abstract No. 9. Rosemont, IL: National Computer Systems.

Slora, K. B., Boye, M. W., & Jones, J. W. (1991). *The construct validity of a work-accident risk measure with MMPI-2 derived scores.* Paper presented at the 26th Annual Symposium on recent developments in the use of the MMPI (MMPI-2 and MMPI-A), St. Petersburg Beach, FL.

Slora, K. B., & Molcan, J. R. (1990). *Psychological organizational risk assessment: A case study.* ESI Research Abstract No. 14. Rosemont, IL: National Computer Systems.

Vernon, H. M. (1918). *An investigation of the factors concerned in the causation of industrial accidents.* Health of Munitions Workers Committee, Memo No. 21.

Wuebker, L. J., Jones, J. W., & DuBois, D. (1985). *Safety locus of control and employee accidents.* Proceedings of the Sixth Annual Industrial/Organizational Graduate Student Conference, University of Akron, Ohio, April 12-14, 1985.

Zuckerman, M. (1971). Dimensions of sensation-seeking. *Journal of Consulting and Clinical Psychology, 36,* (1) 45-52.

Zuckerman, M. (1979). *Sensation-seeking: Beyond the optimal level of arousal.* New York: John Wiley & Sons.

# Slips and Falls in Stores and Malls: Implications for Community-Based Injury Prevention

Donald A. Hantula

Temple University

Jennifer L. DeNicolis Bragger

Montclair State University

Amy K. Rajala

Liberty Mutual Group

**SUMMARY.** An empirical analysis of the behavioral ecology of slip, trip, and fall accidents in grocery stores and shopping malls is presented. The store data set comprised 36 consecutive months of data collected from a chain of grocery stores in the Midwestern USA and the

Donald A. Hantula is with the Department of Psychology, Temple University; Jennifer L. DeNicolis Bragger is with the Department of Psychology, Montclair State University; and Amy K. Rajala is with Performance Technology, Liberty Mutual Group. These data were collected when all authors were affiliated with Temple University. The organizations described in this study were not and are not necessarily past, present, or future customers or suppliers of Temple University, Montclair State University, or Liberty Mutual Group. We in the ivory tower thank our colleagues in the glass tower for their invaluable access and assistance that made this study possible.

Address correspondence to: Donald A. Hantula, Department of Psychology, Weiss Hall (265-67), Temple University, Philadelphia, PA 19122. Electronic mail may be sent via Internet to: hantula@temple.edu.

[Haworth co-indexing entry note]: "Slips and Falls in Stores and Malls: Implications for Community-Based Injury Prevention." Hantula, Donald A., Jennifer L. DeNicolis Bragger, and Amy K. Rajala. Co-published simultaneously in *Journal of Prevention & Intervention in the Community* (The Haworth Press, Inc.) Vol. 22, No. 1, 2001, pp. 67-80; and: *Workplace Safety: Individual Differences in Behavior* (ed: Alice F. Stuhlmacher, and Douglas F. Cellar) The Haworth Press, Inc., 2001, pp. 67-80. Single or multiple copies of this article are available for a fee from The Haworth Document Delivery Service [1-800-342-9678, 9:00 a.m. - 5:00 p.m. (EST). E-mail address: getinfo@haworthpressinc.com].

mall data set included 24 consecutive months of data collected from 22 malls across the continental USA, with a concentration in the southern region. Analyses showed that the majority of the slip, trip and fall accidents occurred on the inside of the establishments, on the same level, and resulted from a water or liquid spill or food item on the floor. Design deficiencies accounted for the least amount of occurrences and cost of the accidents, while housekeeping and inspection deficiencies accounted for the bulk of the accidents. Data-based recommendations for slip, trip and fall injury-prevention strategies in these public places, focusing on management action, are offered. *[Article copies available for a fee from The Haworth Document Delivery Service: 1-800-342-9678. E-mail address: <getinfo@haworthpressinc.com> Website: <http://www.HaworthPress. com> © 2001 by The Haworth Press, Inc. All rights reserved.]*

**KEYWORDS.** Accident cost, accident frequency, behavioral ecology, fall, injury prevention, retail customers, slip, trip

Slips, trips, and falls are a serious, but often-unnoticed, public health problem. According to the National Safety Council (1995), falls account for one-seventh of all accidental deaths and injuries in the USA, claiming approximately 12,000 lives, distributed roughly equally between work and home environments. Ewing and Shensky (1998) contend that one-third of workplace accidents result from slips and falls. Hence, occupational slip, trip, and fall accidents are a growing concern to both safety researchers (e.g., Bentley & Haslam, 1998) and safety professionals (e.g., Bell, 1997; O'Dell, 1998), as are slip, trip, and fall accidents inside and outside of the home (e.g., Fothergill, O'Driscoll, & Hashemi, 1995). In particular, of recent interest to safety professionals are slip and fall accidents in public places such as hotels, restaurants, stores, and malls (e.g, Lewis, 1997; Marshall, 1998; 1999; Smith, 1997), which have important implications for community-based injury reduction efforts. Accordingly, this paper presents an empirical analysis of slip, trip, and fall accidents that occurred in grocery stores and shopping malls in the USA and a resulting series of data-based recommendations for injury-prevention strategies in these public places.

## Walking and Falling

Human walking is known as striding bipedalism, in which each foot carries the center of gravity alternately. Ergonomic research (Lin,

Chiou, & Cohen, 1995) identifies four phases in walking: (1) landing phase, in which the heel strikes the ground; (2) the stationary phase in which the foot is flat on the ground; (3) the takeoff phase in which the front of the foot strikes the ground; and (4) the swing phase in which the foot is passed forward. During the landing phase, support of body weight is transferred from the trailing foot to the leading foot; and momentum carries support of body weight from the heel to toe during the next two phases of walking. During the landing and takeoff phases, only a relatively small part of the foot contacts the ground, and further, when walking, the entire width of the foot seldom contacts the ground. Throughout all four phases, arm swing is used to maintain balance and offset rotation of the body trunk. When the arms are holding objects and cannot swing during walking (as is often the case in a store or mall when holding packages or bags), stability decreases and slips and falls are more probable.

Falling may occur if the walking gait is interrupted by an object (tripping) at any phase, or if the heel strikes the ground during the landing phase and slides forward (slipping), in which there is a high ratio of horizontal to vertical force exerted when the foot contacts the ground (James, 1983). Trips and slips can be averted by altering walking gait, speed and direction to either avoid an object or to adjust to a different floor surface friction; however, if the person cannot detect the object or slippery floor surface in time to make any alterations in walking, a slip, trip and fall may result. In an analysis of fall accidents among the elderly in Europe, Allander, Gullberg, Johnell, Kanis, Ranstam, and Elfors (1998) found that falls on the same level (i.e., not on stairs or other types of elevated surfaces) accounted for over 3/4 of slip and fall accidents and that slipping accounted for nearly half of these same-level accidents. In same-level accidents, it is more probable that slips involving an interruption of the landing phase will result in more serious injury than trips or interruptions of any other phase. Interference with the landing phase often results in continuous pressure placed on the slipping foot, which is more likely to propel the person into a backward fall that can result in serious injuries such as hip fractures, lower back injuries, and concussions. However, with trips or interference with other phases of walking, the person can make quick adjustments in gait or stride, grab for support, or break their fall.

### Behavioral Ecology in Stores and Malls

Sulzer-Azaroff (1978) discusses organizational accident prevention in terms of behavioral ecology; that is, by analyzing behavior, its antecedents and consequences in the natural environment. In this view, slips, trips and falls in stores and malls would not be analyzed by looking for person-based variables such as "accident proneness" but instead by looking for patterns of correlations between environmental conditions in the stores and malls and measures of slip, trip and fall accidents. It may be safely assumed that in the normally-developed adult population, positive consequences for slipping, tripping and falling in a public place are rare; and further that such accidents most likely are not due to knowledge or skill deficits. Thus, an analysis of the natural walking environment, focusing on antecedent conditions of slip, trip, and fall accidents would be the research strategy most likely to yield useful evidence for effective interventions in this particular context.

Consequently, in the following empirical analysis of slip, trip and fall accidents in stores and malls, data on the antecedent conditions extant when the accident occurred are examined for commonalities that could lead to preventive measures. Although slip and fall accidents are a concern in the retail industry, and have accounted for nearly 5% of occupational slip and fall fatalities in the USA during the 1980s (Cattledge, Hendricks, & Stanevich, 1996), the focus in this paper is on retail customers because safety promotion for visitors of these public spaces is more of a community health concern. As food retailing establishments have grown from small grocery stores to supermarkets, they have also increased the number and length of visits by customers, hence the risk of injury. Most importantly, malls have functionally become the new "town centers" of post-industrial life in the USA, serving not only as retail centers but also as sites for dining, entertainment, fitness ("mall walking"), socializing, and community activities; as such they also have become sites of increased injury and risk.

## METHOD

### Data Acquisition

The grocery stores and the malls were insured by one of the largest commercial insurers in the USA. Claims records from a period during the 1990s were examined and all slip, trip, and fall claims were extracted. From the investigated claim reports, the cause of the slip, trip, or fall accident, location, condition of the environment, and amount of money paid for the claim (medical and other costs) were recorded. Cost data provide a rough index of the severity of accidents; a slip which resulted in a soiled piece of clothing would cost less than a slip which resulted in a back injury, thus the combination of the frequency and cost data allow for a more sensitive analysis of these accidents than is obtainable through frequency data alone. Because this study used historical data, the total amount of money paid for claims is included; all claims were "closed." Any claims that may have appeared fraudulent were investigated; no fraudulent claims are included in the data set. The store data set comprised 36 consecutive months of data collected from a chain of approximately 36 grocery stores in the Midwestern USA. The mall data set included 24 consecutive months of data collected from 22 malls operated by the same management company across the continental USA, with a concentration in the southern region. In both cases, the retail spaces were homogeneous in layout and appearance and also in terms of risk management and facilities' management policies and practices.

## *Analysis*

Data were inspected to determine the primary contributing cause of the slip, trip, and fall accident. After common clusters of contributing causes were identified, mean frequency of occurrence by cause and mean cost of injury by cause were computed for each data set. In the mall data set, common clusters of contributing causes were then further classified into a taxonomy of intervention categories (design, housekeeping, inspection, maintenance, other) for further analysis and suggestions for empirically-based interventions.

## *RESULTS*

*Slips and Falls in Stores.* Table 1 shows the cost in USA dollars, number, and proportion of slip, trip and fall accidents in the chain of grocery stores by contributing cause. It can be seen from Table 1 that indoor accidents were by far the most prevalent, and most severe in

TABLE 1. Cost, Number, and Proportion of Slip, Trip, and Fall Accidents in the Grocery Stores by Contributing Cause

| Contributing Cause | Mean (Standard Deviation) Cost in USA Dollars | Number of Accidents | Percent of Accidents |
|---|---|---|---|
| Liquid | 6,416 (16,804) | 93 | 6.3 |
| Nonfood Solid | 6,399 (16,695) | 54 | 3.7 |
| Solid Food | 4,996 (32,434) | 231 | 15.7 |
| Water/Wet Object | 3,897 (18,982) | 407 | 27.6 |
| Grapes | 2,006 (12,743) | 94 | 6.4 |
| Uneven Surface | 1,871 (5,124) | 179 | 12.1 |
| Tripped / No Object | 1,679 (6,918) | 73 | 4.9 |
| Ice/Snow | 1,638 (3,952) | 54 | 3.7 |
| Fall on Curb | 1,022 (2,124) | 52 | 3.5 |
| Fall from Cart | 140 (984) | 194 | 13.2 |
| Fainted | 92 (22) | 3 | .02 |
| Other / Unspecified | 1,679 (9,533) | 73 | 2.8 |

terms of cost per occurrence. Slipping/tripping on water, a wet object, or on a solid food item accounted for a large share of accidents both in proportion of accidents and mean cost per accident. In particular, one food item, grapes, stood out as particularly problematic, accounting for over 5% of all slip, trip, and fall accidents with a mean cost of over $2000 (USA) per incident. Additional analyses showed that indoor accidents accounted for 62% of the accidents and 71% of the cost of injuries.

*Slips and Falls in Malls.* Table 2 shows the cost in USA dollars, number, and proportion of slip, trip and fall accidents in the malls by contributing cause. In contrast to the grocery store data, the mall data show fewer slip, trip, and fall accidents but substantially higher costs for the accidents that occurred. Although falls on escalators were costly, they were relatively rare. However, slipping in water was also costly (over $24K/incident USA) as well as relatively frequent, accounting for 18% of slip, trip, and fall accidents. Tripping on stairs, uneven surfaces, curbs, entrance/exit doors and associated mats or other solid object (e.g., electrical cord, box) collectively accounted for 40% of accidents. Additional analyses showed that indoor accidents accounted for 87% of the accidents and 90% of the cost of injuries. Adults over 35 years old accounted for 59% of the accidents and 82% of the cost of injuries; conversely children 0-12 years old accounted for 22% of the accidents and 6% of the cost of injuries.

TABLE 2. Cost, Number, and Proportion of Slip, Trip, and Fall Accidents in the Malls by Contributing Cause

| Contributing Cause | Mean (Standard Deviation) Cost in USA Dollars | Number of Accidents | Percent of Accidents |
|---|---|---|---|
| Escalator | 45,103 (37,753) | 9 | 3.9 |
| Water | 24,891 (121, 242) | 42 | 18.0 |
| Grease / Oil | 22,163 (168,304) | 7 | 3.0 |
| Fell into Someone | 21,347 (21,292) | 3 | 1.3 |
| Stairs | 11,088 (28,203) | 17 | 7.3 |
| Uneven Surface | 10,227 (30, 851) | 35 | 15.0 |
| Curb | 10,118 (42,105) | 5 | 2.1 |
| Entrance / Exit | 9,723 (20,614) | 10 | 4.3 |
| Solid Object | 6,087 (15,819) | 27 | 11.6 |
| Ice | 6,011 (13,073) | 40 | 17.2 |
| Liquids (other than water) | 5,890 (14,527) | 27 | 11.6 |
| Solid Food | 5,172 (37,577) | 11 | 4.7 |

*Seasonal Variations.* Table 3 shows the data in both stores and malls grouped by season. The distribution of cost per accident and mean number of accidents was fairly even across seasons in the grocery stores but varied greatly in the mall data set. Summer showed a slightly higher mean number of accidents in the stores, while in the malls winter was associated with the highest mean number of accidents, more than twice that of spring or summer. In both the stores and the malls, slip and fall accidents in the Fall evidenced the highest cost per accident. The increase in accident cost during the autumn months is attributable to outdoor accidents involving ice and snow and the upturn in occurrences in malls is to be expected, given the holiday shopping season and its attendant crowds.

*Taxonomy of Intervention Categories–Malls.* Because malls are much larger than grocery stores, have greater heterogeneity of design, are host to people engaging in a wider range of activities, and have become de facto town centers in many communities, it is instructive to review the claim records to determine the common contributing causes of these accidents because these data may speak to more wide-ranging preventive measures. In collaboration with a certified safety engineer, a taxonomy of common contributing causes was developed: design (e.g., slippery floor surface), housekeeping (e.g., food item on floor), inspection (e.g., uneven tile), maintenance (e.g., loose hand-rail), or none determined (sufficient information was not available),

TABLE 3. Mean Cost per Accident in USA Dollars and Mean Number of Slip, Trip, and Fall Accidents in Stores and Malls by Season

| Season | Stores | | Malls | |
|---|---|---|---|---|
| | Mean Cost in USA Dollars | Mean Number of Accidents | Mean Cost in USA Dollars | Mean Number of Accidents |
| Winter | 2,355.36 | 145.00 | 6,164.36 | 42.00 |
| Spring | 2,330.07 | 120.33 | 9,762.63 | 21.33 |
| Summer | 3,330.12 | 162.33 | 14,852.89 | 16.33 |
| Fall | 4,331.80 | 142.00 | 17,224.04 | 24.67 |

and each accident was classified into the category that best fit the description of the incident. Table 4 shows the cost in USA dollars and number of slip, trip and fall accidents in the malls by taxonomy of intervention categories. It can be seen from Table 4 that accidents attributable to deficiencies in housekeeping and inspection accounted for 63% of the occurrences and 89% of the costs; maintenance deficiencies accounted for 1/8 of all accidents but with minimal cost.

## DISCUSSION

An empirical analysis of the behavioral ecology of slip, trip, and fall accidents in grocery stores and shopping malls frequency and severity shows that accidents occurring inside the establishments, largely due to the unanticipated presence of water, other liquid or a food item on the floor, were the most prevalent and overall costly. This study is, to our knowledge, the first analysis of this type focusing on both the frequency and cost of such accidents in a customer population of diverse ages; most research on this topic focuses on either employees (e.g., Bentley & Haslam, 1998) or the elderly (e.g., Fothergill et al., 1995). Consistent with Allander et al. (1998), same-level accidents accounted for the majority of the data; different-level accidents (falling on/from stairs, escalators, curbs) were relatively rare although very costly when they occurred. Winter was the most hazardous season in this sample in terms of accident frequency, due largely to accidents involving ice on the outside and resulting water on the inside, especially around entrance and exit doors. However, autumn proved to be the season with the most costly injuries, perhaps due to the relatively quick changes in weather that can occur between Sep-

TABLE 4. Slip, Trip and Fall Accidents in Malls by Taxonomy of Intervention Category

| Intervention Category | Mean (Standard Deviation) Cost in USA Dollars | Number of Accidents |
|---|---|---|
| Design | 213 (323) | 19 |
| Housekeeping | 8,019 (68,568) | 86 |
| Inspection | 2,189 (6,823) | 60 |
| Maintenance | 446 (1,527) | 56 |
| None | 653 (2,160) | 12 |

tember and November, necessitating equally quick transitions in footwear, which may make for difficulties in adjusting gait or stride when confronted with a sudden slip or trip obstacle.

Ergonomic studies of the biomechanics of walking predict that the most severe slip, trip, and fall injuries should result from interference with the landing phase of walking (James, 1983), which is consistent with the present findings. The most common and costly accidents found in the present study are those that involved a substance such as water, grease or food products which made the floor surfaces more slippery, and more likely to disrupt the landing phase of walking. Further, it would be predicted that laden walking (such as with packages in a mall) would lead to more severe falls because the arms could not be used for balance and motion offset nor to break the fall (Liu et al., 1995). In contrast, laden walking in grocery stores for more than a few steps is rare, and most shoppers use a cart, which can be used for balance or to break a fall. In keeping with these hypotheses, the present study found that same-level accidents in the malls were seen to be more severe than those in the grocery stores in terms of cost.

Preventing slip, trip, and fall injuries is usually discussed in terms of floor surface friction (e.g., Bell, 1997; Bjornstig, Bjornstig, & Dahlgren, 1997; Ewing & Shensky, 1998; Liu et al., 1995; Van Fleet, 1995). Because floor friction is the product of both the floor surface as well as the shoe/foot surface striking it, with employees, an organization can mandate particular footwear with exact tread, sole material, and other safety specifications. However, beyond requiring shoes, the same cannot be demanded of customers. Further, for aesthetic or interior design reasons, slip-prone surfaces (such as marble) may sometimes be preferred to more slip-resistant surfaces (such as rubberized floors or those with serrated surfaces). Thus, interventions focused on modifying floor surfaces, while important and useful in employment environments, may not be as feasible in the consumer environment. However, the present data point to other, potentially more effective areas for intervention that may not be as difficult to implement as floor resurfacing. In the present study, design deficiencies accounted for the smallest percentage of accidents in the malls and the lowest mean cost, suggesting that attention be directed to variables other than floor surface.

Indeed, in both the store and mall data sets, water, other liquids, or food on the floors were the primary contributing causes to the majority of slip, trip, and fall accidents. What this suggests is that independent of floor surface (although floor surface may attenuate or exacerbate the effects of spills), regular upkeep of these surfaces is the critical issue (Marshall, 1998; 1999). This point is reinforced by the mall data in Table 4 showing that deficiencies in housekeeping and inspection resulted in the highest number of accidents, and in the most costly accidents. Further, the housekeeping category also exhibited the most variance in injury cost. Thus, injuries resulting from housekeeping deficiencies would also be those that expose the property owner and insurer to the greatest amount of risk. Intervention strategies focusing on removing spills and debris, alerting customers to their presence, or diverting traffic from spill areas may be the most effective interventions in these public places. People can adjust their walking to avoid or mitigate a hazardous condition, but only if they can detect a hazard. Many spills may be clear or may blend in with the color of the flooring so as to make detection difficult, making simple interventions, including "warning wet" signs or increased lighting of great value in these circumstances.

Combining the behavioral ecology approach of Sulzer-Azaroff (1978) with the present data point to a constellation of prevention strategies focused on the pre-risk and risk phases of the course of injury by means of risk elimination and risk modification (Andersson & Menckel, 1995). If it may be safely assumed that positive consequences for slipping, tripping and falling in a public place are rare and that such accidents most likely are not due to knowledge or skill deficits on the part of the customer, it becomes critical to attend to the physical characteristics of the shopping environment that may facilitate or inhibit these types of accidents. This does not suggest in any way, however, that the role of behavior in these accidents be minimized. Indeed, the data and the discussion thus far point to a much larger recognition of management action and responsibility for preventing slip and fall accidents in stores and malls than may have been previously acknowledged. It appears that the critical issue in slip and fall prevention is not as much one-time design or refurbishing, but ongoing upkeep. That is, slip and fall accidents to occur due to management and/or employee inaction. Regularly inspecting a property for slip and fall hazards, quickly mopping up spills, removing fallen food and grapes, providing entrance mats that absorb water on inclement days, and giving customers clear warning about impending hazardous conditions are all employee behaviors that are directed to a large extent by management.

If management action or inaction is taken as a primary causal variable in preventing slip, trip, and fall accidents, then it is important to specify what types of management action may be the most efficacious in this regard. In a systematic series of behavioral research projects carried out in a hotel chain (Anderson, Crowell, Sponsel, Clark, & Brence, 1982) and a bar (Anderson, Crowell, Hantula, & Siroky, 1988), management actions such as providing clear and unambiguous task clarification and positive consequences for performing specified cleaning activities on a daily or nightly basis were associated with significant improvements in cleanliness. Although neither study focused on slip, trip, and fall accidents as a dependent variable, both studies included increases in floor cleanliness as a dependent measure. In both of these studies, the most important variable in increasing and maintaining cleaning in the establishments was objective feedback from managers given to each employee contingent on their daily performance.

The procedures and results from Anderson et al. (1982, 1988) are consistent with behavior-based safety programs, and when considered in combination with the present data, point to venues for further research and application. Expanding behavioral safety interventions to include environmental variables and employee actions which serve to increase or mitigate potentially hazardous conditions for slip, trip and fall accidents for both employees and customers is a logical first step, as is collecting frequency and cost measures of these accidents (beyond the cleanliness data as in Anderson et al., 1982, 1988) in evaluations of such interventions. Indeed, an entirely unexplored area of behavioral safety concerns customer safety and well-being. Within Industrial/Organizational Psychology as a whole it has become customary to ignore customer-level variables when designing or evaluating safety, or any other "management" interventions (such as employee selection, training) for that matter which has led to a bifurcation in both thought and practice between "management" (employee-focused) and "marketing" (customer-focused) work. Some of this separation can be attributed to evolved specialization; however, the conditions that led to such specialization in the past are not necessarily currently extant. Mechanistic organizational structures, which led to few logical linkages between employee actions and consumer behavior, have been largely replaced by more organic organizational structures that necessitate closer connection between reciprocal actions of employee and customer alike (Hantula, DiClemente, & Rajala, in press). Ironically, the early Industrial/Organizational psychologists worked on both customer and employee issues (DiClemente & Hantula, in press); perhaps we have come full circle.

While the immediate antecedent conditions for slip, trip, and fall accidents were found to be the presence of a foreign slip-inducing substance on the floor, a more distal cause is management action mediated by employee action. Within the limits of these two data sets, it may be advanced that strategies to prevent these accidents in the communities around the stores and malls are managerial in nature. In particular, regular inspection of the physical condition of floors and other walking surfaces and corrective housekeeping action based on these inspections appears to be the most efficacious strategy. Previous research has shown that well-tested managerial actions such as task clarification and feedback (Anderson et al., 1982; 1988) can result in significant improvements in cleanliness. The challenge for future research and application lies in using this knowledge to identify dangerous conditions, train employees to notice potential slip and fall hazards and take corrective action, and managers to provide the appropriate feedback and consequences for maintaining a safe space, and finally to evaluate the impact of these practices on customer behavior, especially safety and satisfaction.

## REFERENCES

Allander, E., Gullberg, B., Johnell, O., Kanis, J. A. Ranstam, J., & Elfors, L. (1998). Circumstances around the fall in a multinational hip fracture prevention study: A diverse pattern for prevention. *Accident Analysis and Prevention, 30*, 607-616.

Anderson, D. C., Crowell, C. R., Hantula, D. A., & Siroky, L. M. (1988). Task clarification and performance posting for improving cleaning in a student-managed university bar. *Journal of Organizational Behavior Management, 9*, 73-90.

Anderson, D. C., Crowell, C. R., Sponsel, S. S., Clark, M., & Brence, J. (1982). Behavior management in the public accommodations industry: A three-project demonstration. *Journal of Organizational Behavior Management, 4*, 33-66.

Andersson, R., & Menckel, E. (1995). On the prevention of accidents and injuries: A comparative analysis of conceptual frameworks. *Accident Analysis and Prevention, 27*, 757-768.

Bell, J. (1997). The best foot forward. *Occupational Health and Safety, 66 (12)*, 26-28.

Bentley, T. A., & Haslam, R. A. (1998). Slip, trip, and fall accidents occurring during the delivery of mail. *Ergonomics, 41*, 1859-1872.

Bjornstig, U., Bjornstig, J., & Dahlgren, A. (1997). Slipping on ice and snow–Elderly women and young men are typical victims. *Accident Analysis and Prevention, 29*, 211-215.

Cattledge, G. H., Hendricks, S., & Stanevich, R. (1996). Fatal occupational falls in the U.S. construction industry, 1980-1989. *Accident Analysis and Prevention, 28*, 647-654.

DiClemente, D. F., & Hantula, D. A. (in press). John Broadus Watson, I/O Psychologist. *The Industrial Psychologist.*

Ewing, L., & Shensky, E. (1998). Careful steps: Mitigating slip and fall liability. *Risk Management, 45 (7)*, 47-52.

Fothergill, J., O'Driscoll, D., & Hashemi, K. (1995). The role of environmental factors in causing injury through falls in public places. *Ergonomics, 38*, 220-223.

Hantula, D. A., DiClemente, D. F., & Rajala, A. K. (in press). Outside the box: The analysis of consumer behavior. In L. Hayes, J. Austin and R. Fleming (Eds.) *Organizational Change*. Reno, NV: Context Press.

James, K. I. (1983). Rubber and plastics in shoes and flooring: The importance of kinetic friction. *Ergonomics, 26*, 83-100.

Lewis, R. (1997). Pier 1's slip-and-fall success. *Occupational Health and Safety, 66 (8)*, 34-38.

Lin, L.J., Chiou, F. T., & Cohen, H. H. (1995). Slip and fall accident prevention: A review of research, practice, and regulations. *Journal of Safety Research, 26*, 203-212.

Marshall, A. (1998). Keep vending areas free from slippery surface hazards. *Hotel and Motel Management, 213 (9)*, 12.

Marshall, A. (1999). Mop up spills so guests can't clean up against your hotel. *Hotel and Motel Management, 214 (1)*, 12.

National Safety Council (1995). *Accident facts*. Itasca, IL: Author.

O'Dell, L. (1998). No slips, no errors. *Occupational Health and Safety, 67 (8)*, 46-49.

Smith, S. L. (1997). Sharing tips on trips and falls. *Occupational Hazards, 59 (5)*, 61-63.

Sulzer-Azaroff, B. (1978). Behavioral ecology and accident prevention. *Journal of Organizational Behavior Management, 2*, 11-44.

Van Fleet, E. L. (1995). Slips, trips, and falls. *National Safety Council Facts and Resources, 1 (2)*, 1-2.

# Individual Differences in Safe Behavior: A Safety Practitioner's Viewpoint

John N. Garis

Garis Safety Training, Inc.

This article reflects upon a number of issues raised in the preceding articles from the viewpoint of a practicing safety and health professional who was not trained as a psychologist. The author has confined comments to his area of expertise which is workplace safety with an emphasis on industrial hygiene and behaviorally based safety training.

## SCOPE OF THE PROBLEM

The National Safety Council publishes an annual statistical compilation of unintentional injuries and fatalities. Unintentional injuries, on and off the job, continues to be the fifth leading cause of death, exceeded only by heart disease, cancer, stroke and chronic obstructive pulmonary disease. The Council (see Table 1) estimates that unintentional injuries also resulted in more than 2.7 million years of potential life lost before age seventy-five in 1996. Using this statistic, unintentional injuries ranks third behind cancer (4.4 million years) and heart disease (3.5 million years; National Safety Council, 1999).

Major efforts are mounted by safety professionals to minimize if not completely eliminate unintentional injuries. Some years they have

---

Address correspondence to: John N. Garis, President, Garis Safety Training, Inc., 1034 Butler Drive, Crystal Lake, IL 60014.

[Haworth co-indexing entry note]: "Individual Differences in Safe Behavior: A Safety Practitioner's Viewpoint." Garis, John N. Co-published simultaneously in *Journal of Prevention & Intervention in the Community* (The Haworth Press, Inc.) Vol. 22, No. 1, 2001, pp. 81-84; and: *Workplace Safety: Individual Differences in Behavior* (ed: Alice F. Stuhlmacher, and Douglas F. Cellar) The Haworth Press, Inc., 2001, pp. 81-84. Single or multiple copies of this article are available for a fee from The Haworth Document Delivery Service [1-800-342-9678, 9:00 a.m. - 5:00 p.m. (EST). E-mail address: getinfo@haworthpressinc.com].

*81*

TABLE 1. Reported Injuries and Fatalities for 1998

| | |
|---|---|
| Disabling injuries | 3,800,000 |
| Number of days of time lost due to injuries | 80,000,000 |
| Unintentional injury deaths | 5,000[a] |
| Costs | $125.1 billion[b] |
| Number of workers | 132,772,000 |

[a] Homicides and suicides are not included in this count.
b Includes wage and productivity losses of $62.9 billion, medical expenses of $19.9 billion, administrative expenses of $25.6 billion, money value of time lost of $12 billion and property damage of $4.7 billion (National Safety Council 1999).

indeed seen improvement only to see the success evaporate the next year when less attention is focused on the problem. Some have reached the point where the accident rate has plateaued because of the reliance on programs. It is what Krause (1997) calls the "accident cycle" and the "performance plateau." Safety practitioners may be left with the feeling, "What are we going to do next?" or "We've tried everything, what are we going to do now?" Thus, it is important to increase options regarding different interventions aimed at improving safety.

## CAUSES OF ACCIDENTS

Accidents are more accurately labeled as disabling events and can be attributed to one of three causes as depicted in Figure 1. These causes can be categorized into person, environmental and behavior factors. Person factors are those internal factors such as knowledge of hazards, attitudes, opinions, internal motivations and physical fitness. Environmental factors are the conditions that come into play in the workplace such as machine guarding, trip and fall hazards, standard operating procedures, manufacturing and management systems. Safety professionals often group these under the heading of *unsafe conditions*. The third leg of the triad is individual behavior.

Most of the papers in this collection are focused on the person factor leg of the triangle and/or measurement issues as related to safe behavior and accidents. It should be noted that other important areas related to safety exist beyond the scope of this volume, which constitute the majority of safety interventions.

FIGURE 1. Causes of Accidents

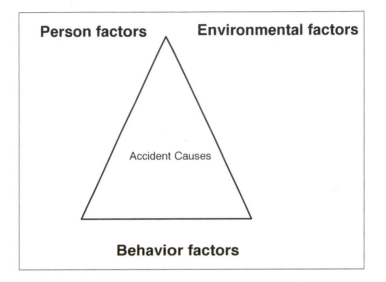

Person factors    Environmental factors

Accident Causes

Behavior factors

## *INDIVIDUAL DIFFERENCES AND PRACTICE*

The author agrees with Smith et al. that most near miss incidents go unreported but could provide important information that could prevent future debilitating accidents. W. H. Heinrich demonstrated in the late thirties and early forties that for every serious disabling incident there would be a multiple of non-disabling or near miss events and an even larger multiple of events leading up to the near miss and serious disabling event. However, because of the administration of workers' compensation systems and the federal regulations, industry in the United States tends to be reactive rather than proactive to the event. To get to prevention, safety practitioners should be more proactive in identifying the cause prior to the disabling event. Other than the airline industry and the military, near miss reporting and investigation is rarely done. The author believes accidents have rational, identifiable causes. Accidents are a progression of a sequence of events. Remove several of the events out of the chain and the accident will not occur. Thus the measurement and documentation of near misses may be critical in preventing disabling events.

The individual difference research presented is encouraging but caution is in order. The results seem to identify certain characteristics related to accident involvement but issues of faking and employee reaction should not be ignored. It should also be noted that expertise is required in the development, administration and interpretation of such measures. Thus, a safety practitioner such as myself would need to work with other professionals with expertise in assessment and employment testing. However, any gain in the prediction and understanding of disabling accidents will likely prove worthwhile.

## *CONCLUSIONS*

In order for a safety program to be as effective as possible it must integrate personal, environmental and behavioral factors into a control mechanism aimed at reducing disabling events. In the field, behavior management aimed at hazard identification, job observation, positive and corrective feedback and reinforcement has increased safe behavior and reduced accidents (NATLSCO, 1996). This is consistent with other behaviorally based safety training programs (e.g., Geller, 1996). This research certainly adds to the understanding of accident causation and if implemented appropriately, to the overall effectiveness of safety programs.

## REFERENCES

Geller, E.S. (1996). *The psychology of safety*. Radnor, PA: Chilton.

Krause, T. (1997). *The behavior based safety process*. New York: Van Nostrand Reinhold.

National Safety Council. (1999). *Injury facts*. Itasca, IL: NSC.

NATLSCO. (1996). *Safe behavior management processes*: *Instructors' guide and participants' guide*. Long Grove, IL: National Loss Control Service Corporation.

# Index